So What
Does God Have
to Do with
Who I Am?

Joey O'Connor has worked in youth and family ministry for fifteen years in Southern California. He is a conference speaker and the author of thirteen books for couples, parents, and young adults. He lives with his wife and four children in San Clemente, California, where he likes to surf, eat fish tacos, and lie in the hot sand.

His works include:

You're Grounded for Life! & 49 Other Crazy Things Parents Say

Have Your Wedding Cake and Eat It Too: You Can Be Happy and Married

I Know You Love Me, but Do You Like Me? Becoming Your Mate's Best Friend

Women Are Always Right & Men Are Never Wrong

Heaven's Not a Crying Place: Teaching Your Child about Funerals, Death, & the Life Beyond

In His Steps: The Promise

Excuse Me! I'll Take My Piece of the Planet Now

Whadd'ya Gonna Do? 25 Steps for Getting a Life

Breaking Your Comfort Zones

Graffiti for Gen X Guys by J. David Schmidt with Joey O'Connor

Graffiti for Gen X Girls by J. David Schmidt with Joey O'Connor

For speaking events, conferences, and seminars, call 1-877-447-4377. You can also write to Joey O'Connor at P.O. Box 3373, San Clemente, CA 92674-3373. Visit Joey's web site at http://www.joeyo.com. You can e-mail Joey with your comments and questions at:

joey@joeyo.com

So What Does God Have to Do with Who I Am?

Joey O'Connor

Fleming H. Revell
A Division of Baker Book House Co
Grand Rapids, Michigan 49516

Published by Fleming H. Revell
a division of Baker Book House Company
P.O. Box 6287, Grand Rapids, MI 49516-6287

Printed in the United States of America

Library of Congress Cataloging-in-Publication Data

O'Connor, Joey, 1964–
    So what does God have to do with who I am? / Joey O'Connor.
        p.   cm.
    ISBN 0-8007-5753-X
    1. Teenagers—Religious life. 2. Teenagers—Conduct of life.
3. Christian life—Biblical teaching. [1. Christian life.] I. Title.
BV4531.2.O38   2001
248.8'3—dc21
                                               2001019702

For current information about all releases from Baker Book House, visit our web site:

http://www.bakerbooks.com

To my beautiful, fun, and creative daughter,
Janae Nicole O'Connor:

May you always know the truth of who you are
and the wonder of God's love for you.

Contents

Introduction   9

Part One: A True Original   13

Selfishness • Conformity • Self-Acceptance
• Negative Thoughts • Comparing Yourself to Others
• Making Good Decisions • Strength in Weakness
• Living God's Way • Being Unique

Part Two: Why Me?   45

Disappointment • Angry at God • Attitudes
• Living beyond Regret • Life's Not Fair • Getting
the Blame • Self-Pity • Questioning God • Taking
Responsibility • Evil in the World

Part Three: What God Says   77

God's Promises • God's People • Forgiveness
• Life and Death • Counting on Jesus • God's
Love • God's Word • God's Goodness • God's
Presence • Persisting in Prayer

Introduction

Have you ever not wanted to bother God because he seemed like an Einstein, too brilliant and too busy to be concerned with your puny problems? Isn't the gospel supposed to be simple to understand? Why don't people talk about God in terms that everyone can grasp?

God wants you to know who he is and what he is like, and you don't need to go to night school or take a fifty-two-week language course to understand him or the Bible. Below are some BIG words in simple, user-friendly language that'll help you. You'll discover that he isn't too complicated or too busy to listen to you. He has all the strength you need, and his attention is focused on helping you develop a better relationship with him. God is . . .

Omnipresent. From Mars to Bangkok to Button-willow to Madagascar, God is everywhere. He doesn't need Frequent Flyer programs to get from here to there in First Class or Coach, because he cannot be limited to a location or place. God is everywhere. That means he can help you wherever *you* are.

Omnipotent. God is all-powerful when it comes to strength and making the impossible possible. He can handle any problem you toss at him and lift it off your shoulders quicker than an Olympic weight lifter.

Omniscient. Wouldn't you love to sit next to God in class? He knows everything! There is no secret, wonder, mystery, idea, math problem, thought, or question that is hidden to him or that he doesn't already have the answer to. God is all-knowing, and there is nothing he doesn't understand. He understands your questions, doubts, fears, dreams, and struggles. He has the knowledge and wisdom to give you the right advice even before you ask him.

Sovereign. Kings, presidents, dictators, and rulers will come and go, but God is the supreme ruler over everything. He has the exclusive authority and power over choice real estate like Newport Beach, the Milky Way, and every other piece of property in the universe. No human decision or situation is beyond his ability to control or affect his ultimate purposes. For those who trust and love him, he promises to work all problems toward good, not harm.

Eternal. Who said it better than Jesus himself: "I am the Alpha and the Omega, the First and the Last, the Beginning and the End" (Rev. 22:13). You can have hope in God and in his eternal presence, because he promises that he will always be with you. He'll never leave you or tell you to take a hike. He always was, always is, and always will be. God is with you now and for eternity.

Immutable. God isn't like you and me; he doesn't have good days and bad days. He never changes. He's always the same. God isn't affected by moods, atmospheric conditions, ecological disasters, or tidal changes. He will always help you, understand you,

Introduction

and love you, and he promises to walk with you no matter how difficult your problem may be.

Infinite. God is beyond limitations, measurements, sizes, and conceptions. In other words, if you try to keep God in a box by nailing it shut and wrapping it with duct tape, you shouldn't be surprised when the box begins to shake. God's powerful presence will be with you during times of depression, pain, and sorrow. He won't make your life problem-free or remove you from difficulties he can use to help you grow closer to him. Either way, you can depend on him to give you an infinite amount of strength to hang in there.

The Scripture verses listed in this book are meant to offer you hope, encouragement, and peace; they are not meant to be a cure-all for any and every problem. There is a very real danger in using the Bible as a mask to cover or deny problems. Some people misuse Scripture by believing that in simply repeating a Bible verse, God's Word becomes a magical pixie dust that erases all their problems. God's Word tells us to confront problems, not run from them. When you read a verse listed, look it up in your Bible so you can discover the context in which it's written. If you have further questions, talk to your parents, youth pastor, church leader, or friend. Study God's Word responsibly. He gave it to us to accomplish his purposes. It is not a tool to accomplish our own purposes or a shield to hide from our problems.

God's Word was written to develop a foundation for our lives (see Matthew 7:24-27), lives that are wholeheartedly lived in, through, and for God. Therefore, all Scripture is used to build that foundation. Not just one verse. God is interested in you becoming a whole person, and he uses the whole Bible to speak to you. One or two isolated verses are not enough to build a foundation for your life any more than one or two bricks are enough to construct a house. The purpose of this book is to show you that God's Word is absolutely relevant in every area of our lives. Let this book stimulate you to read the Bible. Ask yourself, "How can what I'm reading help me to better know and love God so I can serve him in every area of my life?"

1

A True Original

Before I was married, my friends and I often headed to Santa Barbara on the weekends to surf and visit friends. After finishing a great surf session one beautiful Saturday morning, we sat down for breakfast and watched the breaking waves from our restaurant table. The sun warmed our cool skin as we looked over our menus; we were ready for a big meal. Suddenly, at the table next to us, a pretty, young girl wearing sunglasses caught my eye. She looked familiar, but I couldn't figure out where I had seen her before. I noticed that she had a set of crutches and was sporting a full-length cast on her left leg. "Where have I seen her before?" I kept asking myself. She wasn't hard on the eyes, but there wasn't anything too remarkable about her. As I kept wondering where I knew her from, she sat by herself looking at some slides she had in her hand.

It finally came to me. Trying to be very cool and not too obvious about it, I leaned over and whispered to my friends, "Dana! Bobby! Look at the table in back of you. It's Kathy Ireland!"

"Kathy who?" they replied.

"Kathy Ireland, the girl from the *Sports Illustrated* swimsuit editions. I know it's her. Turn around and look, but . . . but don't make a scene!"

Bobby and Dana turned around, looking to see if my discovery was true and said, "I don't know, Joey . . . are you sure?"

"Yes, I'm sure. Look, she even has slides of her photos."

Sure enough, as we debated back and forth whether or not this was indeed the Kathy Ireland of *Sports Illustrated* fame, two girls (obviously friends) arrived at her table and said, "Hi, Kathy! How's it going? Are those new photos of you?"

Every day hundreds of thousands of young people gasp and gaggle over the high-paid models of today's modern fashion and fitness magazines. Billions of dollars are spent each year in advertising budgets to woo you into buying whatever's being served up in the latest cosmopolitan cafeteria of creature comforts. What's wrong with this picture? Somehow, I've got a sneaking suspicion you and I aren't getting the whole picture when we see cover girls and cover guys. When was the last time you saw a gorgeous blond with a full-length cast on the front cover of *Cosmopolitan?* Have you ever seen a model on the cover of *Seventeen* with sweat running down her face from the glaring heat of the photo session lighting? It's been said that the camera never lies. If the camera never lies, then who's telling the truth?

Being consumed with buying the latest clothes, having our hair just right, and looking like Mr. or Miss Universe can cause us to forget that we are true originals. God's originals. When we forget that we are God's originals, that we are fearfully and wonderfully made (see Psalm 139), three things can happen.

1. *We begin to believe that outer beauty is more important than inner beauty.* Television, movies, and magazines constantly

A True Original

bombard young people with the notion that you're not enough. You're lacking something. You don't measure up. I say, "Don't buy the lie." The One who made you to be a true original says this: "The LORD does not look at the things man looks at. Man looks at the outward appearance, but the LORD looks at the heart" (1 Sam. 16:7). Focusing on outer beauty can often lead to insecurity, eating disorders, poor self-esteem, and depression. It can lead us to believe that being pretty or handsome is more important than who we are on the inside.

2. *We play the comparison game.* Believing that outer beauty is more important than inner beauty can also lead us to comparing ourselves to others. It's called the comparison game. I play it; you play it; we've all played it at one time or another. The game works like this:

When you compare yourself to others, you either make yourself superior or inferior to the other person. And neither of these two things is a godly characteristic. When you play this game, you will always lose.

3. *We forget God says that we are true originals.* If everyone tries to copy one another because of ruthless comparisons, then nobody's an original . . . everyone becomes a black-and-white Xerox copy! Who wants to be a copy of a copy of a copy? God has gifted you; you are like a painter's palette full of colors. You have your own mind, thoughts, feelings, and personality. If you spend all your time and energy on how you look or on comparing yourself to how others look and act, you'll forget that you are a unique creation of God. You have a personality that no one else has had or ever will have. Out of the 98,125,872,531,635,892 quadzillion people that have walked the face of the earth, there is no one else like you! You are a true original! God has designed a place in his kingdom just for you. You are special, loved, and created

for a very specific purpose. God wants to paint your life with the colors of his love.

Kathy Ireland only tore a few ligaments in her knee. Knees heal a lot quicker than hearts that have been torn up by the comparison game. Comparing yourself to others is a merry-go-round that's hard to get off, but God is a God of grace and compassion. As you ask him to help you develop your inner beauty, a personality that reflects Christ's love, he will show you that you are fearfully and wonderfully made. Your personality, developed into the character and heart of Christ, will never need crutches and a cast to help it stand on its own.

Selfishness
A Big, Fat, Selfish Pig

Oink! I once had a fetal pig named "Piggy Sue." She and I met when I was a senior in high school. My anatomy and physiology teacher introduced us. He said Piggy Sue needed a place to live, and I offered my mom's refrigerator at home. Our first date was a dissection. When I was picking Piggy Sue's brain on what life was like as a pig, she just kind of stared at me. (You know, the way girls do when they're infatuated.) Over the course of the semester, Piggy Sue and I became really good friends. But there was one thing about pigs I didn't understand. A friend had always told me, "Pigs don't sweat, they wallow." I never knew what he meant, but now was my chance to find out. One day I popped the big question: "Piggy Sue, I know this is kind of personal, but could you tell me why your kind wallows in the mud?" She stared at me. No response. The next day, Piggy Sue broke up with me.

That was the last dissection I'll ever date, but since then, I've learned why pigs wallow in the mud: They don't have sweat glands. Pigs can't sweat. To keep from baking to death and exploding sausage and bacon all over the place, pigs roll around in the mud to cool themselves. These swine don't wallow for nothing. It's in their nature to wallow. Pigs wallow to survive.

Humans are a lot like swine. Just like pigs don't have sweat glands, our nature is to think of "me" before "you." We don't have it in us to be natural givers. That's selfishness. It's what the Bible calls sin. God's Word helps us become more like his Son, Jesus, and less like animals that wallow. He knows it's not in our natural self to think of others first. That's why he gives us a completely new nature in Christ. When you wallow in yourself, you give off an odor that repels others. That stinks. But if you live in the new nature God gives you, you probably won't get skinned alive for being a pig.

I'm always wanting more and more "stuff"; how can I make God the center of my life and not be so materialistic?

Turn my heart toward your statutes and not toward selfish gain.

PSALM 119:36

HOW TO KEEP YOUR EGO IN CONTROL

Disclaimer: The acts of cruelty you will soon read about were performed by a trained professional. None of these acts should be attempted in your home unless you desire to be grounded for life. The author who carried out these dastardly deeds is thirty-seven years old, and his parents still have him restricted to his room with absolutely no phone privileges.

When was the last time you were cruel? I mean, really cruel? Not just mischievous or kidding around but a deliberately mean-to-the-core, everything you had in you C-R-U-E-L?

(There's more!!)

☞

When I was a teenager, I came very close to perfecting the subtle yet calculated art of cruelty. Ask John Vopale. He got a broomstick through his bike spokes while going down a hill. Ouch! That's cruel. Or ask my younger sister, Loretta. She wasn't able to go to the eighth-grade dance at my school because I told our next-door neighbor not to buy her a ticket. Not until after spending the entire afternoon shopping for a new dress and getting her hair styled did Loretta discover there was no ticket for her . . . an hour before the dance started. That's really cruel. Aside from other minor acts of cruelty like shooting people in the rear with my BB gun, putting my dissected fetal pig in my sister's bed (when you have five sisters and one little brother, you need to resort to creative means of self-preservation), and water-blasting the drive-up window lady at Jack-in-the-Box with a fire extinguisher, cruelty was as much a part of my life as blood in my veins.

I grew up thinking it was cool to be occasionally cruel. I never joined a gang or got arrested for shoplifting or stole a Plymouth Horizon . . . I was actually a pretty good kid. Simply put, at times, I was a jerk. For me, acting "cool" was more important than others' feelings. (Or should I say, physical

(Read on!!)
☞

How can I keep from always trying to make myself look better than others?

Do nothing out of selfish ambition or vain conceit, but in humility consider others better than yourselves.

PHILIPPIANS 2:3

I lent some money to this guy I don't like, and now he won't pay me back; how should I react?

"And if you lend to those from whom you expect repayment, what credit is that to you? Even 'sinners' lend to 'sinners,' expecting to be repaid in full. But love your enemies, do good to them, and lend to them without expecting to get anything back. Then your reward will be great, and you will be sons of the Most High, because he is kind to the ungrateful and wicked."

LUKE 6:34–35

How can I keep from resenting friends who get all the lucky breaks?

But if you harbor bitter envy and selfish ambition in your hearts, do not boast about it or deny the truth.

JAMES 3:14

Sometimes I feel like a slave to selfishness; how can I break free?

For we know that our old self was crucified with him so that the body of sin might be done away with, that we

Selfishness

should no longer be slaves to sin—because anyone who has died has been freed from sin. Now if we died with Christ, we believe that we will also live with him.

ROMANS 6:6–8

My friends and I are always trying to outdo each other; will our friendships suffer because of it?

For where you have envy and selfish ambition, there you find disorder and every evil practice.

JAMES 3:16

How can I keep my selfishness from getting in the way of following Jesus?

Then he said to them all: "If anyone would come after me, he must deny himself and take up his cross daily and follow me. For whoever wants to save his life will lose it, but whoever loses his life for me will save it."

LUKE 9:23–24

How can I become more like Christ?

You were taught, with regard to your former way of life, to put off your old self, which is being corrupted by its deceitful desires; to be made new in the attitude of your minds; and to put on the new self, created to be like God in true righteousness and holiness.

EPHESIANS 4:22–24

safety . . . I wonder if John's still in the hospital?) I had an ego that sometimes got out of control. An ego out of control is one that is too cool to care what others think or feel. Do you ever have an ego that's out of control? Do you do things that are "too cool" regardless if you hurt a family member, girlfriend, boyfriend, or people you don't even know?

Well, what are some of the stupid "too cool" things we do to massage our out-of-control egos? Let's start with ego breath. The words we use in the name of coolness can often be a horrendous stench to others. Put-downs such as "You've got enough zits on your face to grease a hundred axles!" can evaporate relationships quicker than you can spell ego.

Our actions, both subtle and not so subtle, are another way we communicate our interest in ourselves rather than our interest in others. We've both seen it and/or done it. Take the jock, for instance, who emits a godlike aura when he struts around waiting for his coach, girlfriend, and mom to heed his every need. And what about making fun of people you think are unattractive? Have you stopped to consider that what you say and do can destroy people God says are made in his image?

(See page 21.)

☞

Conformity
Being God's Person

One of the biggest challenges you face as a teenager is deciding whether you should conform to God's standards or the world's standards. The world's standards are the thoughts, attitudes, and actions that go against who God wants you to be. God wants to transform your life so you can be the unique person he's meant you to be. The world wants to press you into a cookie-cutter mold. God has made you to be an original. He isn't into stamp sets, photocopiers, or assembly-line production.

Conforming to what everyone else wants you to do robs you of your originality. It makes you like someone else instead of yourself. The fear of discovering who you are can cause you to conform to others. But how can you be sure others know who they really are? If everyone is conforming to each other, then no one knows who they really are. (UGH!) In other words, the horses may be on the merry-go-round, but they're just spinning in circles and their legs ain't moving. This is one monotonous, meaningless merry-go-round you can dismount.

In the Book of Galatians Paul shows us that he has discovered who he is in Jesus Christ: "I have been crucified with Christ and I no longer live, but Christ lives in me. The life I live in the body, I live by faith in the Son of God, who loved me and gave himself for me" (Gal. 2:20). Paul understands that God has made him to be like no one but Christ. Is that conformity? Yes.

Is that meaningless? No. Developing and growing in a friendship with Jesus Christ can help you discover who you are in God's family. Jesus Christ has given you talents and abilities like no one else's. And he wants to give you a friendship no one else can. Conforming to the attitudes and actions of what everyone else is doing hurts this friendship. Living the way God specifies in his Word strengthens who you are in Christ. Conforming your life to Christ transforms who you are. Conforming to the world's standards confines you to be someone you aren't. What's it gonna be?

I dyed my hair and bought a whole new wardrobe just to be different; the only problem is I don't feel any different about myself. What does God's Word say about this?

Do not conform any longer to the pattern of this world, but be transformed by the renewing of your mind. Then you will be able to test and approve what God's will is—his good, pleasing and perfect will.

ROMANS 12:2

Will God keep me from going back to my old ways?

As obedient children, do not conform to the evil desires you had when you lived in ignorance.

1 PETER 1:14

I don't understand why so many of my Christian friends have fallen away from God. Is this common?

Why do we do these things? Why are our attitudes programmed to believe that it's cool to be cruel? Please press the "pause" button on your ego right now and let's be honest about why we do the stupid things that we do.

1. Acceptance. We all want to have friends and be liked by others. Our need for acceptance is so strong it can easily outweigh the pain others will suffer from our words and actions. For most teens, guys especially, it's easier to be cruel than to look stupid. Cruelty, however, isn't gender specific. In order to win acceptance, some girls spread rumors about someone they don't like.

2. Affirmation. In high school and junior high, guys get applause for who can be "grosser than gross" or "crueler than cruel." If you pick on a little twerp half your size, you can win the laughter and smiles of your buddies. It's a lame system, but among some types of friends, cruelty gets extra credit.

3. Apathy. Who gives a rip? "I'll do what I want to do when I want to do it and to whomever I want!" Sometimes we're cruel because we purposely choose to be cruel. We really

(There's more!!)

☞

don't care about others because we're too busy thinking about ourselves. That's a dangerous ego. An ego out of control.

The only thing an ego out of control will do for you is make you conceited, unapproachable, and self-centered rather than others-centered. In God's eyes, that's very uncool. However, an ego that is in control, one that is focused on Jesus Christ, is cool. In God's eyes, VERY COOL. In Philippians 2:3–5, Paul writes, "Do nothing out of selfish ambition or vain conceit, but in humility consider others better than yourselves. Each of you should look not only to your own interests, but also to the interests of others. Your attitude should be the same as that of Christ Jesus." Before Paul was a Christian, he thought he was cool . . . extremely cool. Paul's ego was so out of control he thought it was cool to murder Christians—throw 'em into jail, then kill 'em. Paul was cruel. But when he got knocked to the ground by God, he quickly found out that he and dirt had a lot in common. (Take a look at Acts 9.)

Meeting Jesus face-to-face is what it took to cool down Paul's ego. Although Paul

(Check out the oval!!)

☞

> People will be lovers of themselves, lovers of money, boastful, proud, abusive, disobedient to their parents, ungrateful, unholy, without love, unforgiving, slanderous, without self-control, brutal, not lovers of the good, treacherous, rash, conceited, lovers of pleasure rather than lovers of God.
>
> 2 Timothy 3:2–4

I know I'm supposed to conform to God's plan, but how can I know his purpose for my life?

> For it is God who works in you to will and to act according to his good purpose.
>
> Philippians 2:13

Will God help me not conform to my friends when they want me to do bad things?

> With this in mind, we constantly pray for you, that our God may count you worthy of his calling, and that by his power he may fulfill every good purpose of yours and every act prompted by your faith.
>
> 2 Thessalonians 1:11

Conformity

It's easy for me to believe that God exists, but what will my friends think if I really make up my mind to follow Christ?

Yet at the same time many even among the leaders believed in him. But because of the Pharisees they would not confess their faith for fear they would be put out of the synagogue; for they loved praise from men more than praise from God.

JOHN 12:42–43

I want to conform to God's will, but what should I do when I get tired of hanging in there?

Finally, brothers, we instructed you how to live in order to please God, as in fact you are living. Now we ask you and urge you in the Lord Jesus to do this more and more.

1 THESSALONIANS 4:1

Should I rely on the Holy Spirit's power to help me live the way God wants me to?

Those controlled by the sinful nature cannot please God. You, however, are controlled not by the sinful nature but by the Spirit, if the Spirit of God lives in you. And if anyone does not have the Spirit of Christ, he does not belong to Christ.

ROMANS 8:8–9

probably spent the rest of his life getting the sand out of his nostrils, he gave us some great advice to help us keep our egos in control.

• **Don't be selfish.** Next time you and your ego begin to battle it out, ask yourself, "Am I being self-centered or others-centered like Jesus Christ?"

• **Be humble.** It's easy to brag about our accomplishments. Instead of lifting yourself above others, find out a few things others have done right and brag about them.

• **Discover the interests of others.** A sure way to win friends is to be sincerely interested in what interests them. Discovering what others think is important shows them that you think they're important.

• **Think like Jesus.** The writer of Proverbs was right, "As a man thinks in his heart, so is he." Whatever you think about, you will often end up doing. If you think about yourself most of the time, you'll be selfish. Developing a closer relationship with Jesus will help you think like Jesus. It will change your attitudes about how you treat people, what you say, and how you live your life. Jesus wasn't into cruel. He was into being cool. Very cool. Not your way or my way. God's way.

(That's all!!)

Self-Acceptance

Acceptance, with One Exception

Am I Okay? Accepting yourself for who you are is pretty hard to do if you haven't figured out who you are in the first place. What if you did find out who you really were, only to be disappointed at what you found? Or scared? Or repulsed? Or shocked?

Many students today have no problem accepting who their friends are. They like their friends' personalities, the way they dress, their interests, sports, and music. Most students like anything about their friends. The only exception to how accepting they are is that, when it comes to liking themselves, they make an exception.

"I can accept others, except myself." It's amazing how two words can sound so similar but be continents apart in meaning. According to the *American Heritage Dictionary,* to accept someone means to "receive gladly." When was the last time you gladly received yourself? Or does this next one hit you in the gut: *Except* (as a verb) means to "exclude or leave out." I know a lot more students who exclude themselves than I do students who gladly receive who God has made them to be.

When God thinks of you, he gladly receives you as his child. He has great plans for your life. He can help you accept yourself even when you don't like what you see. He wants you to discover who you are in him, because you were designed to reflect his image. That's an image worth reflecting. It doesn't matter what you've done or how awful you think you are, God receives and doesn't exclude. With God, there are no exceptions.

Why do I have such a problem accepting myself and consequently accepting others?

Accept one another, then, just as Christ accepted you, in order to bring praise to God.

ROMANS 15:7

Did people in the Bible ever feel rejected by God?

You are God my stronghold. Why have you rejected me? Why must I go about mourning, oppressed by the enemy? Send forth your light and your truth, let them guide me; let them bring me to your holy mountain, to the place where you dwell.

PSALM 43:2–3

Did Jesus ever get rejected like I do? And did he ever feel different from everyone else like I do?

He then began to teach them that the Son of Man must suffer many things and be rejected by the elders, chief priests and teachers of the law, and that he must be killed and after three days rise again.

MARK 8:31

He was despised and rejected by men, a man of sorrows, and familiar with suffering. Like one from whom men hide their faces he was despised, and we esteemed him not.

ISAIAH 53:3

Does God accept me even if I don't have much to offer him?

"I took you from the ends of the earth, from its farthest corners I called you. I said, 'You are my servant'; I have chosen you and have not rejected you."

ISAIAH 41:9

Being Alone with God

My daughter Janae is much older now, but this scenario, written when she was two, is still relevant. So, here goes.

One of my favorite things about being a daddy is when my little girl, Janae, climbs up on my lap. The big, leather reclining chair in our house is "Daddy's chair." It doesn't matter what time of day it is, but whenever I'm doing my boring adult stuff like reading the paper or a favorite book, I've got about 3.8 seconds before Janae vrooms over, yanks my arm, and says, "Stam up, Daddy! Stam up!" Whenever she's in a "stam up" mood, she either wants to do airplane, go for a short walk to look for the neighbor's cat that doesn't have a tail, or have me be a lizard chasing her across the

(Keep reading!)

☞

room. If Janae isn't in a rambunctious "stam up" mood, she runs to her bookshelf and grabs her favorite assortment of reading literature. Classics like *Where the Wild Things Are, The ABC Animal Book,* and *Encyclopedia Britannica, A–M* (she hasn't gotten past "M" yet . . . she's only two!). She scampers up on my lap and says, "Come on, Daddy, read!" It's then when the warmth and softness of Daddy's chair carries both of us into a fantasy world of pictures, dreams, and make-believe. Janae, sitting quietly on Daddy's lap, listens to big words and dramatic sounds. Before her brown, wonder-filled eyes, stories come alive, the characters jumping out of the pages to play with her in her daddy's lap.

When was the last time you sat in your daddy's lap? No, not your real dad . . . your heavenly dad! Psalm 131:1–2 says, "My heart is not proud, O Lord, my eyes are not haughty; I do not concern myself with great matters or things too wonderful for me. But I have stilled and quieted my soul; like a weaned child with its mother, like a weaned child is my soul within me."

God loves you like his very own child. He wants to spend time with you, telling you about the dreams, stories, and adventures he has in the friendship you can share together. Sitting quietly in his lap away from the craziness and stress of everyday life will

(Check out the circle on the next page!)

☞

Does God accept me just as I am?

"I will restore them because I have compassion on them. They will be as though I had not rejected them, for I am the Lord their God and I will answer them."

ZECHARIAH 10:6

How can I know God won't reject me?

As you come to him, the living Stone—rejected by men but chosen by God and precious to him—you also, like living stones, are being built into a spiritual house to be a holy priest-hood, offering spiritual sacrifices acceptable to God through Jesus Christ.

1 PETER 2:4–5

　　　　　　　　　　　Self-Acceptance

Negative Thoughts

Monkey See, Monkey Do

Get Real! Have you ever been to the monkey exhibit at the zoo? Those crazy primates most likely have a lot more fun staring at a group of weird-looking tourists and their young than we do staring at them. So who's laughing at whom? Are the cages to protect the humans from the monkeys or the monkeys from the humans? Unlike humans, monkeys are very honest about how they feel. If they don't want you around, they hurl handfuls of monkey waste to motivate you to move to the next exhibit. I've always wondered why they don't throw banana peels instead.

Our thoughts are a lot like monkeys staring back at us. They can keep to themselves or they can torment us with their antics. Jumping up and down in our brain, screeching, fighting, and throwing dung at us can wreak havoc on our self-image. Their shrill screams can make us cringe. Or their playfulness can make us feel as if we're likable. Either way, there's not enough room in our head for human brains and monkey brains.

God can silence the monkeys in your brain by replacing your anxious thoughts with his peace. It's easy to get crunched with King Kong pressures, doubts, and frustrations. God's power can cage any ape trying to make banana mush out of you. "He will not let your foot slip—he who watches over you will not slumber" (Ps. 121:3).

give you peace like nothing else. When you're alone with him, he wants to whisper in your ear, "You're my favorite one. There's no one else like you. I love you." Because you are an original, you are his favorite. God's love is so wide, so high, and so deep that nothing can ever separate you from his love. If you're feeling like nothing special or like no one has a special love for you, spend some time in your heavenly daddy's lap. He's got plenty of room for you.

(That's all!!)

I've got a lot of stuff on my mind; will God help me clear my thoughts?

Listen to my prayer, O God, do not ignore my plea; hear me and answer me. My thoughts trouble me and I am distraught.

PSALM 55:1–2

Does God really know what I'm thinking?

You know when I sit and when I rise; you perceive my thoughts from afar.

PSALM 139:2

My thoughts toward others haven't been very nice, but I want to change. Will God forgive me for being so negative?

Let the wicked forsake his way and the evil man his thoughts. Let him turn to the LORD, and he will have mercy on him, and to our God, for he will freely pardon.

ISAIAH 55:7

Why doesn't the Bible talk about the way God thinks?

"For my thoughts are not your thoughts, neither are your ways my ways," declares the LORD. "As the heavens are higher than the earth, so are my ways higher than your ways and my thoughts than your thoughts."

ISAIAH 55:8–9

My mind gets bombarded with all sorts of bad thoughts; how can I focus on God better?

Therefore, holy brothers, who share in the heavenly calling, fix your thoughts on Jesus, the apostle and high priest whom we confess.

HEBREWS 3:1

How can I apply God's Word to what goes through my mind?

Negative Thoughts

"Fix these words of mine in your hearts and minds; tie them as symbols on your hands and bind them on your foreheads."

DEUTERONOMY 11:18

My attitude has been pretty bad lately; how can I change my attitude and be the person God wants me to be?

You were taught, with regard to your former way of life, to put off your old self, which is being corrupted by its deceitful desires; to be made new in the attitude of your minds; and to put on the new self, created to be like God in true righteousness and holiness.

EPHESIANS 4:22–24

All I think about are things that concern me; how can I include God in what I'm thinking?

Set your minds on things above, not on earthly things.

COLOSSIANS 3:2

Comparing Yourself to Others

No Comparison

When you're shopping for a car stereo, a mountain bike, or any other item, comparing prices is important. It takes more time, but you can save big bucks. Comparing is also real important when you want to buy two similar products. Like liverwurst and headcheese. I know it's tough deciding between the two, but it's important to compare lest you buy the unhealthier of the two. Gag!

A True Original Test

You're an original, but do you really believe it? Take a few minutes to answer these somewhat weird and original questions to discover how God has made no one else like you. Let the results remind you that God takes pride in his original works of art. (That's you!)

1. Write down the name of someone identical to you. (Note: Identical twins can skip ahead to the next question.)
2. Look at your hand for fifteen seconds (wiggle fingers, flex open and closed, make a peace sign). Write down the name of someone with the exact number of hairs on each of your fingers.
3. Scribble ink on your thumb and make a thumbprint on a

(There's more!!)
☞

Comparing is great when you're shopping. But in relationships, comparing is like playing Russian roulette with a loaded gun. You never win. Whenever you compare yourself with others, you always lose. Why? Either you come out better than the other guy (not God's way), or you come out worse than the other guy (not God's way either). Each way creates pride, jealousy, envy, and a poor self-image. The Bible says not to compare yourself to someone else so you won't fall into something reserved for God: judgment. Judging others against yourself and vice versa causes you to make evaluations that aren't yours to make. There's always going to be someone prettier, smarter, funnier, or stronger than you are. God doesn't compare you to anyone else, because you are his unique creation. You are one of a kind. He created you to be compassionate like Jesus. If there's one comparison you can make, compare yourself to Jesus. He'll make you to be all that you feel you're not. In shopping, comparison saves. In relationships, comparison kills.

Why do I always come out the loser when I compare myself to others?

We do not dare to classify or compare ourselves with some who com-

Comparing Yourself to Others

mend themselves. When they measure themselves by themselves and compare themselves with themselves, they are not wise.

2 CORINTHIANS 10:12

Where is God when I feel worthless?

"Indeed, the very hairs of your head are all numbered. Don't be afraid; you are worth more than many sparrows."

LUKE 12:7

My best friend is always competing with me, and it gets me really angry; how can I keep from falling into the same trap?

Make sure that nobody pays back wrong for wrong, but always try to be kind to each other and to everyone else.

1 THESSALONIANS 5:15

I get my priorities mixed up when I compare myself to others; what can I do?

"But seek first his kingdom and his righteousness, and all these things will be given to you as well."

MATTHEW 6:33

What's more important: inner beauty or outer beauty?

Your beauty should not come from outward adornment, such as braided hair and the wearing of gold jewelry and fine clothes. Instead, it should be that of your inner self, the unfading

piece of paper. Go to the FBI and ask them to do a nationwide search for someone with your identical thumbprint. Write down the name of this person.

4. Go into the bathroom, look closely in the mirror and count the number of brown freckles on your nose (freckles only, no blackheads). Write down the name of someone with the exact number of brown freckles on their nose.

5. Sneeze. Give the precise velocity, time span, and loudness of your sneeze. Write down the name of someone who produces the exact same type of sneeze as you.

6. Go to the dentist. Have him x-ray your teeth. Go back to the FBI. This time, ask them to do a DRS (Dental Records Search). Write down the name of the person who matches your canines and bicuspids.

7. (You'll need a couple friends to help you with this one.) Count the number of hairs on your head. If you lose count, you may want to start over by pulling them out, one at a time. Write down the name of the person who is half-bald like you.

8. Look at the whites of your eyes. Count the number of veins in both eyes. Write

(Turn the page!!)
☞

Comparing Yourself to Others

down the name of the person who has the exact number of veins as you.
9. List three extraordinary qualities about yourself. Write down the name of the person who has the exact same three.
10. Read Psalm 139 and list the incredible things said about you. Write down the name of the person who wrote these great things about you.

(That's all!!)

beauty of a gentle and quiet spirit, which is of great worth in God's sight.

1 PETER 3:3–4

There's this guy in class who doesn't have much money, and my rich friends tease him all the time. What should I do?

He who despises his neighbor sins, but blessed is he who is kind to the needy.

PROVERBS 14:21

Can God drown out all the negative comparisons that are made about me?

"The LORD your God is with you, he is mighty to save. He will take great delight in you, he will quiet you with his love, he will rejoice over you with singing."

ZEPHANIAH 3:17

I've got a friend who's always nervous about what others think of her. How can I help her out?

An anxious heart weighs a man down, but a kind word cheers him up.

PROVERBS 12:25

Making Good Decisions
Personal Choices

"It's my choice; I have the right to do anything I want!" This attitude runs rampant through our country, like a beaver at a lumber sale. So many people want to do their own thing regardless of how it affects others. They want rights but no responsibility, choices without consequences, freedom without faithfulness. It seems people have forgotten that their rights, their choices, their decisions have a powerful impact on the lives of others. What they say, what they do, and who they are sends tremendous ripples into the current of our society.

In the Book of Hosea (chapter 4), Hosea wept and mourned in despair when all he saw in his country was cursing, lying, and bloodshed. No one wanted to know God. They wanted all their rights, choices, and personal freedoms at the cost of their faith. They wanted choices without consequences. They wanted pleasure instead of his presence. They wanted power instead of peace. Bummer.

In thinking about the choices you make, keep these things in mind: (1) God has a heart. When you make choices that distance you from God, you not only hurt yourself, you hurt God. The very God who loves you and wants your friendship. Poor choices create poor relationships. (2) Think about others. What about your family? Would your choices embarrass them? What about your friends? Would your choices hurt them in any way? What about others who may be looking to discover a friendship with Jesus, but you may be the one God wants to use? Will your choices affect their decision to follow Christ?

It's hard to make good choices if you view God like a judge ready to clobber you with a galaxy gavel. But if you know God as a close friend, someone who really cares about you, good choices deepen that friendship. Instead of you alone, it's God and you. Those choices become very personal for both you and God.

Making Good Decisions

Rebel with a Cause

Rebellion is IN. Being a unique individual is the way to stand out in a crowd. Whoever dresses the ugliest, dyes their hair the most bizarre color, cuts or grows it the exact opposite of what their parents like, is honored with the coveted N.C.C.A. (Nonconforming Conformist Award). Nonconforming is a big deal until everyone looks like everyone else. Then everyone gets bored. In the sixties, rebellion was a big thing. James Dean. Janis Joplin. Jimi Hendrix. All rebels. All dead. All without a cause. And for what? Long hair? Bell-bottom jeans? Psychedelic Volkswagen vans that broke down a lot? Rebellion doesn't get people very far. Now or then.

Growing up is a time to accept yourself for who you are. Enter rebellion. A lot of young people think they need to rebel in order

(Read on!!)
☞

I'm struggling with my faith; why should I keep following Christ?

"Now choose life, so that you and your children may live and that you may love the LORD your God, listen to his voice, and hold fast to him. For the LORD is your life."

DEUTERONOMY 30:19–20

Where is God when it's easy for me to get pulled away from him because I'm so materialistic?

Choose my instruction instead of silver, knowledge rather than choice gold.

PROVERBS 8:10

Does God tempt me to see if I'll choose to do the right thing or not?

When tempted, no one should say, "God is tempting me." For God cannot be tempted by evil, nor does he tempt anyone; but each one is tempted when, by his own evil desire, he is dragged away and enticed.

JAMES 1:13–14

I get so frustrated trying to choose between right and wrong. Why can't I just do the right thing all the time?

I know that nothing good lives in me, that is, in my sinful nature. For I have the desire to do what is good, but I cannot carry it out.

ROMANS 7:18

Making Good Decisions

to be an individual. To do that, teenagers throw away things they think they don't need anymore. Barbie dolls. G. I. Joes. Parents. Teachers. Or anybody else who tells them what to do or believe. Rebellion is doing the opposite of what someone else wants you to do. Most young people want to make their own decisions about what to believe and whom to choose as friends. Without Mom or Dad. Rebellion is a lot more popular than MTV. Your parents can unplug the TV, but they can't unplug you.

Rebellion isn't a new concept. Adam and Eve were rebellious gardeners. David was a murderer who blew off God. He made most teenage rebellion look like chopped liver. And where were the disciples when Jesus was hanging on the cross? Desertion City. The Bible reminds each one of us that rebellion has been around for a long time. We have all blown off God.

If you're in the process of trying to figure out who you are by becoming an individual, you can rebel without blowing off God or your parents. Think about this: Never rebel against someone who would die for you. Would the crowd you're hanging out with actually die for you? Would they step in front of a forty-ton freight train or speeding semi so that your life could be spared? Looking cool may be important, but dead is not cool. Even a rebel will tell you that. So why hang out with people who are trying to figure out who they are at your expense? Rebellion has a price, but nobody wants to pay it.

(Don't stop here! See page 37.)

☞

How can I remind myself to keep following God's ways and not my own?

Yes, LORD, walking in the way of your laws, we wait for you; your name and renown are the desire of our hearts.

ISAIAH 26:8

Why can't I see immediate results from making good choices?

The desire of the righteous ends only in good, but the hope of the wicked only in wrath.

PROVERBS 11:23

I've been hanging out with a bunch of guys known for making trouble; is that bad?

Do not envy wicked men, do not desire their company.

PROVERBS 24:1

I really want to do what God wants me to do; how can I put him first in making good decisions?

I desire to do your will, O my God; your law is within my heart.

PSALM 40:8

Strength in Weakness

When I'm Weak, Then I'm Strong

Way Cool!! Sometimes when you're experiencing a tough problem, you feel like you're alone on a deserted island surrounded by man-eating sharks. Everyone else seems to be cruising by on their yachts, kicking back in the sun, waiting for lunch to be served while you're picking sand out of your teeth. You're alone. No one understands. Everyone else is doing just fine.

Weakness isn't something that our society holds in high regard. Images of having sand kicked in your face, being picked on by bullies, and looking like a geek are the stuff of old comic book ads. It's not cool to cry or show how you really feel in today's world. At school, you've got to appear cool, composed, and totally with it to make it in the eyes of others. When you're going through a problem, how is it possible to drop your guard and let others see you're hurting?

It takes a lot of guts to be honest and risk being weak when others may not understand. Even in youth groups, where it "should" be okay to be weak, it's usually not. After all, you're supposed to be a strong Christian. Jesus understands what it's like being weak. Jesus made himself to be weak regardless of what others thought of him. That was pretty risky. When he was sad at the death of his friend Lazarus, he wept.

When he was bummed out, he took time away from others to pray. Jesus understood the weakness of human beings because he understood the effects of sin. Sin makes us weak, and that's why he came to die for us. He made himself weak so that we could be strong in him. Paul the apostle was overcome and depressed by his weakness, but God said to him, "My grace is sufficient for you, for my power is made perfect in weakness" (2 Cor. 12:9). God knows we can't be strong on our own. That's why his grace is enough. It's enough to make us strong, and it's enough to help us understand it's okay to be weak in his strength.

I feel so lame that I don't know how to pray better. Can God help me?

In the same way, the Spirit helps us in our weakness. We do not know what we ought to pray for, but the Spirit himself intercedes for us with groans that words cannot express.

ROMANS 8:26

How should I reply when my friends say it's foolish to believe in God?

Questioning authority is not wrong. Wanting to be an individual isn't wrong either. God has designed you to be an individual who understands his design for your life. Too often though, students want to chuck God, chuck parents, chuck everything in order to be an individual. Rebellion and individuality are not the same thing. Rebellion is running from God. Individuality is being who he designed you to be. If you want to be an individual, blowing off God or trashing your relationship with your folks isn't the way to do it. You can be an individual without rebelling, but rebelling won't make you an individual.

So how can you be a rebel with a cause? ('Cause you want to know and love God but you still have a few questions . . . 'cause your parents aren't as bad as they seem . . . 'cause you want good friends and not jerks for friends.) Micah 6:8 offers a three-part answer to a simple question: "And what does the

(One more box to go!!)
☞

For the foolishness of God is wiser than man's wisdom, and the weakness of God is stronger than man's strength.

1 CORINTHIANS 1:25

Strength in Weakness

LORD require of you? To act justly and to love mercy and to walk humbly with your God." If you really want to be an individual and not just another rebel, ask yourself, "Am I acting justly in all I say and do?" A rebel couldn't care less about treating people right. An individual has the courage to act God's way. "Do I love mercy?" Rebels can be merciless. They're more interested in themselves than others. An individual who loves mercy is someone who feels good enough about himself or herself to show forgiveness toward others. "Am I walking humbly with God?" Which direction are you walking?

Some time ago I conducted a funeral for a student who died in a rock-climbing accident. Death brings rebellion close to home. It makes me wonder, "Is rebelling against Jesus Christ, the very one who died for my sin, really worth it?" Are you rebelling? Are you running from God? Rebellion can make you an individual, but it can also make you very lonely. If you're going to rebel, rebel against the things that are not just, not merciful, or that keep you from walking humbly with God. In God's eyes, that's rebellion with a cause.

(That's all!)

Did Paul ever feel scared as a Christian?

I came to you in weakness and fear, and with much trembling.

1 CORINTHIANS 2:3

Sometimes I'm overwhelmed trying to be a "good Christian." Does God accept my weaknesses?

Therefore I will boast all the more gladly about my weaknesses, so that Christ's power may rest on me.

2 CORINTHIANS 12:9

Will God give me power to overcome my weaknesses?

For to be sure, he was crucified in weakness, yet he lives by God's power. Likewise, we are weak in him, yet by God's power we will live with him to serve you.

2 CORINTHIANS 13:4

I feel like I'm slipping away from God; how can I hang on?

He is able to deal gently with those who are ignorant and are going astray, since he himself is subject to weakness.

HEBREWS 5:2

I'm so limited in my understanding of God's power. Can he show me how powerful he is?

Strength in Weakness

You are the God who performs miracles; you display your power among the peoples.

PSALM 77:14

I've heard all there is to hear about being a Christian, but I want to see it in action; is that possible?

For the kingdom of God is not a matter of talk but of power.

1 CORINTHIANS 4:20

I wonder: Is it God's power or my own that keeps me walking with him?

But we have this treasure in jars of clay to show that this all-surpassing power is from God and not from us.

2 CORINTHIANS 4:7

Living God's Way
You Gotta Do Right

Choose, Dude! Right or wrong? Wrong or right? What about right and wrong? Can you have both? This life is filled with endless choices about doing the right or wrong thing. What you choose is up to you, but what you choose also comes back to you. No, I'm not talking about karma or reincarnating into a blind gnat. Jesus said you can tell a tree by its fruit. A good tree produces good fruit and a bad tree makes rotten apples. What kind of fruit are you producing? People will be able to tell who you are by looking at the produce section of your life. If you want to produce good fruit, you gotta do right. If you produce bad fruit, it's because you're doing wrong.

What you do, right or wrong, will affect how you feel about yourself. People who constantly do wrong are usually insecure, selfish, and unsure about who they really are. People who do right things do so because they know why they're choosing to do right. In other words, it's easy to do wrong. Anyone can do it. It doesn't take much creativity or effort. But to do right takes a willful, deliberate choice. That type of choice produces good fruit. The type of fruit that Jesus said would last.

What are some ways to serve others?

"Stop doing wrong, learn to do right!
Seek justice, encourage the oppressed.
Defend the cause of the fatherless,
plead the case of the widow."

ISAIAH 1:16–17

How can I change my attitude about poor people?

He who oppresses the poor
shows contempt for their Maker,
but whoever is kind to the needy
honors God.

PROVERBS 14:31

I've had countless talks with a friend about the bad stuff he's doing, but he won't listen to me. Can I do anything to change him?

"Let him who does wrong continue to do wrong; let him who is vile continue to be vile; let him who does right continue to do right; and let him who is holy continue to be holy."

REVELATION 22:11

I need help understanding how to do what's right. Can God's Word help me?

For the word of the LORD is right and true; he is faithful in all he does.

PSALM 33:4

My friend doesn't believe that people sin; what can I tell her?

Living God's Way

There is not a righteous man on earth who does what is right and never sins.

ECCLESIASTES 7:20

Some of my friends "say" they're Christians, but they act completely the opposite; are they really Christians?

Dear children, do not let anyone lead you astray. He who does what is right is righteous, just as he is righteous.

1 JOHN 3:7

I get so confused; how can I figure out if I'm following God or not?

This is how we know who the children of God are and who the children of the devil are: Anyone who does not do what is right is not a child of God; nor is anyone who does not love his brother.

1 JOHN 3:10

I realize that what I've been doing is wrong; will God help me change?

Let us examine our ways and test them, and let us return to the LORD.

LAMENTATIONS 3:40

Does God remember my past sins?

"Their sins and lawless acts I will remember no more."

HEBREWS 10:17

Being Unique

You're Thumbody

Be You. Do you ever feel like a thumb? The odd person out? Or just a plain oddball? Weird? Different from everybody else? Or maybe too unique? There are a lot of unique things in this world that people don't want to get close to: two-headed snakes, dogs foaming at the mouth. Scary, weird stuff.

If you feel too unique, it's crucial to remember that in God's eyes, you can never be too unique. Or too special. In God's eyes, you're unique because that's the way he made you. He is a master designing a wonderful creation. You are his masterpiece in the making. You may feel like a wandering appendage to the earth's crust, but you make a difference to God. Being special to God is as real as your thumb being connected to your hand. The thumb is a critical part of the hand. Without it, it'd be impossible to pick up spare change, grip ski poles, shake hands, or do thumb wars. You're unique. You're special. And there's no one in the whole world like you.

My friends at youth group say I'm a good speaker; how can I keep my ego from getting in the way?

"Let him who boasts boast in the Lord."

2 CORINTHIANS 10:17

I'm not very talented; will God help me discover what I can do?

"If you then, though you are evil, know how to give good gifts to your children, how much more will your Father in heaven give the Holy Spirit to those who ask him!"

LUKE 11:13

A lot of my Christian friends have been talking about their "spiritual gifts." How can I discover what mine are?

Since you are eager to have spiritual gifts, try to excel in gifts that build up the church.

1 CORINTHIANS 14:12

Being Unique

Why didn't God give me the same gifts and abilities my friends have?

We have different gifts, according to the grace given us.

ROMANS 12:6

How can I figure out what my role in the church is?

And in the church God has appointed first of all apostles, second prophets, third teachers, then workers of miracles, also those having gifts of healing, those able to help others, those with gifts of administration, and those speaking in different kinds of tongues.

1 CORINTHIANS 12:28

I'm depressed because I feel like I have nothing to offer God; will he help me get out of this problem?

"And I will do whatever you ask in my name, so that the Son may bring glory to the Father. You may ask me for anything in my name, and I will do it."

JOHN 14:13–14

God has given me many abilities; how can I use them to share my faith with others?

"In the same way, let your light shine before men, that they may see your good deeds and praise your Father in heaven."

MATTHEW 5:16

Why Me?

Don't you just love it when something bad happens to someone you can't stand? How about when the weird-looking guy in your math class gets blamed for something he didn't do and everybody laughs at him? Or when the sleazy girl whose locker is next to yours gets caught for drinking? How about when the jerk on the football team gets kicked off the squad and you suddenly get promoted from second-string to first-string? Isn't it great to see your enemies, the people who drive you nuts, get made fun of? Teased? Put on suspension? Become the butt of every joke? Isn't it wonderful for them to discover, the hard way, that the world doesn't revolve around them?

Life is sweet when the sugar's in our bowl. But when things go sour, stale, or downright rotten, life can leave a bitter aftertaste. The typical whine we're all familiar with goes something like this: "These other people get what they deserve, but I'm not like them. Why is this happening to me?" When life throws you a wild curveball, it's easy to get caught standing too close to the plate. You try to duck, but the stinking ball smacks you upside the head. You wonder: Why'd that have to happen to me? How come I'm the one who always gets nailed? How come nothing like this happens to anyone else?

If you're feeling like a target, then welcome to the ball club; we're all targets. Life is one big fastball, and eventually, we're all going to get hit. That doesn't mean God is the Greg Maddox of the universe. Even though he's been around for a long time, he's not trying to peg you. "Well, if God really loves me, then why does he allow bad things to happen to me?" you might ask. God is not a baseball pitcher. He's not a referee. He's not a third-base coach telling you when to go for home or play it safe. God is God. He is who he is. As he said himself, "I AM WHO I AM" (Exod. 3:14).

When you're thinking *Where in the world is God?* or *Why me?* remember that, just as the world doesn't revolve around your enemies who get what they deserve, the world also doesn't revolve around your own little cosmos. "'For my thoughts are not your thoughts, neither are your ways my ways,' declares the LORD. 'As the heavens are higher than the earth, so are my ways higher than your ways and my thoughts than your thoughts'" (Isa. 55:8–9). For reasons beyond my ability to explain to you, God allows certain things to happen because he is God. His thoughts are not your thoughts. His ways are not the way you would do things. He operates on a different agenda than you and I do.

God loves you exactly for who you are. Now that's a wild way of operating. In Romans 5:8, Paul talks about God's crazy way of running this world: "But God demonstrates his own love for us in this: While we were still sinners, Christ died for us." When you're wondering "Why me," remember that God never says, "What makes you so special? Why not you?" He always says, "I love you." If anyone had a reason to ask "why me," it was Jesus Christ. When Jesus was dragging his cross through the streets of Jerusalem, he could have gone kicking and screaming the whole way. He could have yelled to the people laughing at him along the road, "You think this is fair? I'm getting a raw deal here! Why are you blaming everything on me? I didn't do anything."

During any given day, you may grumble at God and wonder why he allows you to eat the raw end of the hot dog. Jesus understands what it's like to get a raw deal; he is God's answer to all your whys. He may not explain why your favorite pet died, why you failed a test, why your best friend had to move away, why people can be so mean, why you get mistreated, or why you have the problems you do. You cannot know all of God's thoughts or reasons, but you can know his heart. You can know that he says he'll never leave or forsake you. You can know that nothing can separate you from his love. You can know that he's with you when everyone else has abandoned you. Why? Because Jesus knows what it's like to be abandoned. Jesus knows what's behind your whys. He knows what it's like to say why.

When Jesus was hanging on the cross, alone, with no one to help or comfort him, he asked God why: "About the ninth hour Jesus cried out in a loud voice, 'Eloi, Eloi, lama sabachthani?'—which means, 'My God, my God, why have you forsaken me?'" (Matt. 27:46). Jesus knows why.

Disappointment

Did God Let Me Down?

Check It Out! Life is filled with disappointments. Disappointment with friends. Disappointment with family. Disappointment with broken dreams. Disappointment with God. When things don't go as planned or turn out how you thought they would, it's easy to feel like God let you down. You might be asking, "If God really loves me, then why did my boyfriend break up with me? How come bad things happen only to me? Doesn't God want me to be happy?"

Thinking that God let you down or feeling as if he really doesn't care about you is something that many teenagers experience. Feeling alone, like no one understands, struggling all by yourself, and wishing things were different can separate you from a loving God who loves and cares for you. Even when you are disappointed with God, he understands why. He does allow us to experience pain. He lets us go through deep, dark, lonely valleys. God doesn't promise to take away problems. He promises his presence in the midst of problems. When you experience disappointment with God or feel abandoned by him, he wants you to recognize that he is with you. When I'm frustrated or disappointed with God, it's usually because I'm frustrated with myself. Instead of running to him for help, I tend to blame him for my problems. Sound familiar? You and I will always let ourselves down, but God is always there to pick us up. He promises us his presence, his peace, his rest.

Will God ever disappoint me?

"Then you will know that I am the LORD; those who hope in me will not be disappointed."

ISAIAH 49:23

When I'm scared to face my fears, will God help me out?

"Have I not commanded you? Be strong and courageous. Do not be terrified; do not be discouraged, for the Lord your God will be with you wherever you go."

JOSHUA 1:9

I've had it easy, but now my life is really hard, and I wonder, has God let me down?

"Consider now: Who, being innocent, has ever perished? Where were the upright ever destroyed? As I have observed, those who plow evil and those who sow trouble reap it."

JOB 4:7–8

Where is God when I need his help?

Hear, O Lord, and be merciful to me; O Lord, be my help. You turned my wailing into dancing; you removed my sackcloth and clothed me with joy.

PSALM 30:10–11

I used to be a really strong Christian, but now I feel flat and empty. How can I get out of this discouraging period in my life?

So my spirit grows faint within me; my heart within me is dismayed. I remember the days of long ago; I meditate on all your works and consider what your hands have done.

PSALM 143:4–5

I've prayed and prayed for God to help me with temptation; why am I still struggling?

FIFTEEN WAYS TO EXTRICATE YOURSELF FROM EMBARRASSMENT

You were a Science 101 phenom. Nobody could ignite a Bunsen burner better than you. I mean, like who had memorized the genus and phylum of all the indigenous plants and small critters within three square miles of your school? And who had to constantly correct your science teacher when it came to the biochemical structure of subatomic selenium particles? Tell me, please tell me, who else had a chromium, nonstatic pocket protector capable of holding multicolored markers, Dixon Ticonderoga #2 soft lead pencils, and a special wireless device (that you created!) that could send

(Read on!!)

☞

No temptation has seized you except what is common to man. And God is faithful; he will not let you be tempted beyond what you can bear. But when you are tempted, he will also provide a way out so that you can stand up under it.

1 CORINTHIANS 10:13

Why don't I seem to be as confident in God as I used to be?

For you have been my hope, O Sovereign LORD, my confidence since my youth. From birth I have relied on you; you brought me forth from my mother's womb. I will ever praise you.

PSALM 71:5–6

I'm disappointed because God hasn't answered my prayers quick enough. Is he ignoring me?

Listen to my prayer, O God, do not ignore my plea; hear me and answer me. My thoughts trouble me and I am distraught.

PSALM 55:1–2

Angry at God

Growing beyond Bitterness

Have you ever been in a fight with a friend who refused to make up and go on with life? The friend was so hurt, so angry, so bitter at you that forgiveness wasn't in his or her vocabulary. Instead of dealing with the problem, the person ignored your constant attempts at solving the conflict and tragically split your friendship in two. God knows how you feel. This type of stuff happens to him all the time.

God has a lot of people ticked off at him. A lot of angry, frustrated, enraged, bitter people who blame him for their lousy families, one-point losses, car crashes, bad grades, and ruthless teachers. These people refuse God's friendship for even the slightest of problems. Instead of seeing God as a tender and loving Father who created them, they often shake their fists at him and scream "Why?"

Growing beyond bitterness is impossible with a clenched fist. God opens his hand to you in friendship to walk with you every day of your life. Do you want to live a bitter, angry life? Bitterness leaves an awful taste in your soul. Bitterness will poison your relationship with God and the people in your life. How long can you stay angry at God? Pry open your fingers and accept his friendship. Then decide what type of friend you are going to be.

Can God soften my heart when it has been hardened by bitterness?

"I will give you a new heart and put a new spirit in you; I will remove from you your heart of stone and give you a heart of flesh."

EZEKIEL 36:26

and receive e-mail to the cafeteria? You were known as the . . . *Science Stud. Molecular Macho Man. Internet Icon. Einstein on the Prowl.*

That is, until you accidentally dropped your dissected, eviscerated kitty cat on the homecoming queen's lap when you slipped on a petri dish. You fell hard on the yellow linoleum floor. The cat's claws stuck to her skirt. She screamed bloody murder as if the cat was attacking her, causing a horrific chain reaction of similar catastrophes throughout the science room. And the photographer for the school newspaper captured it all on film.

Looking for a creative way to extricate yourself out of this thoroughly embarrassing moment? Here is what you need to do to save yourself in this dastardly situation and any others in your fatalistic future.

(There's more!!)

☞

I need to be freed from past hurts and bitterness. Will God heal me if I ask him?

"If you, then, though you are evil, know how to give good gifts to your children, how much more will your Father in heaven give good gifts to those who ask him!"

MATTHEW 7:11

Is it okay to tell God how I really feel about my struggles?

"Therefore I will not keep silent; I will speak out in the anguish of my spirit, I will complain in the bitterness of my soul."

JOB 7:11

I don't want to die a bitter, unhappy person. Can God help me be at peace with myself when I die?

"One man dies in full vigor, completely secure and at ease, his body well nourished, his bones rich with marrow. Another man dies in bitterness of soul, never having enjoyed anything good."

JOB 21:23–25

What should I do when I find myself getting bitter?

Get rid of all bitterness, rage and anger, brawling and slander, along with every form of malice.

EPHESIANS 4:31

I've got a friend who's really bitter at me; how do I fix the problem?

David was greatly distressed because the men were talking of stoning him; each one was bitter in spirit because of his sons and daughters. But David found strength in the LORD his God.

1 SAMUEL 30:6

Where is God when I feel like blowing him off? Can it really be that bad not following him?

"Your wickedness will punish you; your backsliding will rebuke you. Consider then and realize how evil and bitter it is for you when you forsake the LORD your God and have no awe of me," declares the Lord, the LORD Almighty.

JEREMIAH 2:19

1. Be a hero. Grab the Bunsen burner and pretend to fight off the ferocious kitty.
2. Play dead. (You might as well . . . you won't have a life after this stunt.)
3. Blame the homecoming queen. No one will believe you, but it's worth a try.
4. Claim a new scientific discovery.
5. Call the Center for Animal Abuse. Seek an indictment against your school.
6. Jump to your feet and scream, "An alien made me do it! An alien made me do it!"
7. Ask the photographer to take a picture of you, the cat, and the homecoming queen.

(One more!!)
☞

8. Stand up. Brush yourself off. Play it cool. Say, "Has anyone seen my cat?"
9. Tell the homecoming queen she should be thankful for this learning opportunity.
10. Seize the moment: Ask her out on a date.
11. Ask your parents and principal for permission to transfer schools.
12. Blame the homecoming queen #2: Yell, "She's wearing fur! Animal hater!"
13. Writhe on the floor and act seriously injured. Perhaps someone will feel compassion.
14. Play up the Batman theme: *Look! It's Catwoman!*
15. Think of ways to exploit this opportunity to give the Science Club greater exposure.

(That's all!)

A friend of mine was hurt by other Christians and is really bitter about it. How can I help him?

See to it that no one misses the grace of God and that no bitter root grows up to cause trouble and defile many.

HEBREWS 12:15

Attitudes

Raw Deal #1

Raw deals. Nobody orders them, but everybody gets them. When you get a raw deal, the one thing you need to watch out for is the poisonous bacteria that comes inside. Just like salmonella in chicken or makayupuke in sushi, raw deals can poison your attitude.

A friend of mine once said, "Things break, bodies bruise, and personalities clash. Remember these three things and you'll never be disappointed." In other words, life is filled with raw deals. Expect 'em and you won't be surprised. He was right. Why should we be surprised with broken fingernails, flat tires, speeding tickets, bad calls, bird droppings on our head, stolen teddy bears, and being treated unfairly or being ignored?

Bad attitudes equal bad living. Jesus Christ came to give us abundant life. Not a problem-free life but security, peace, confidence, and hope through a relationship with him. Raw deals don't have to produce bad attitudes. You can choose how to deal with your raw deal. You can let God carve your character into the image of Christ as he helps you grow closer to him.

What should I do when my faith's been shaken because other Christians were mean to me?

Surely he will never be shaken; a righteous man will be remembered forever.

PSALM 112:6

Is trying to be honest really worth it?

The truly righteous man attains life, but he who pursues evil goes to his death.

PROVERBS 11:19

How should I react when I'm always getting blamed for things I didn't do?

For though a righteous man falls seven times, he rises again, but the wicked are brought down by calamity.

PROVERBS 24:16

How can I change my attitude after getting pegged for something that wasn't my fault?

Through Jesus, therefore, let us continually offer to God a sacrifice of praise—the fruit of lips that confess his name.

HEBREWS 13:15

Where is God when I'm sick of getting raw deals?

In your struggle against sin, you have not yet resisted to the point of shedding your blood.

HEBREWS 12:4

All my problems seem meaningless; does God have a purpose for them?

Endure hardship as discipline; God is treating you as sons. For what son is not disciplined by his father?

HEBREWS 12:7

I get picked on just because I'm small; does Jesus understand what I'm feeling?

He was oppressed and afflicted, yet he did not open his mouth; he was led like a lamb to the slaughter, and as a sheep before her shearers is silent, so he did not open his mouth.

ISAIAH 53:7

For we do not have a high priest who is unable to sympathize with our weaknesses, but we have one who has been tempted in every way, just as we are—yet was without sin. Let us then approach the throne of grace with confidence, so that we may receive mercy and find grace to help us in our time of need.

HEBREWS 4:15–16

I'm always overlooked for promotions at work. Does God notice me?

Helping friends in Trouble

I once got a phone call from a girl in our youth ministry with a serious problem. She was wondering what to say to a group of friends who wanted her to go to Magic Mountain. Going to Magic Mountain wasn't the problem. Her friends wanted to use acid while they were at the park. Getting their stomachs turned inside out wasn't enough. They wanted to do the same with their brains.

If you're stuck in the middle of a difficult conflict with a friend, it's easy to say, "This is just great. Why did I get dragged into this problem?" Helping friends in conflict is a delicate art. If you're in a situation with a friend who's in trouble, but you're not exactly sure what to do, here are some important ideas that can help you under-

(Keep reading!!)
☞

But the eyes of the LORD are on those who fear him, on those whose hope is in his unfailing love.

PSALM 33:18

Living beyond Regret

A Second Chance

Should have. Would have. Could have. Making poor decisions can result in guilt, regret, and ugly consequences. Looking back at what we should have done, would have done, or could have done can be agonizing. *I should have kept my eyes on my own paper. I would have studied harder if I'd have known the test was going to be so hard. I could've gotten by with a "C." Now I've got detention and an "F" for cheating.*

Thank God that he gives second chances. And third chances. And fourth chances. . . . In his goodness and forgiveness, he graciously gives us more chances than we ever deserve. He wants to turn our shoulds into obedience, our woulds into a desire for right living, and our coulds into a strong commitment to follow Jesus. Just because God forgives and forgets our sin doesn't mean he condones or likes our mistakes. It shows how great his love is for us. Just like anyone else, he doesn't want to be taken for granted. He wants our hearts and lives returned to him in grateful response for all he does for us. If you feel like you've let others, yourself, or God down by making some bad decisions, you've been given a second chance by God. Don't take him for granted. He loves you more than you can imagine. Just give your life to him every day and take your second chance.

I regret walking away from God and messing up our friendship. Will he take away my feelings of guilt and regret?

Godly sorrow brings repentance that leads to salvation and leaves no regret, but worldly sorrow brings death.

2 CORINTHIANS 7:10

I feel like I'm still paying for something I did wrong a long time ago. How can I get beyond this?

"Sow for yourselves righteousness, reap the fruit of unfailing love, and break up your unplowed ground; for it is time to seek the LORD, until he comes and showers righteousness on you."

HOSEA 10:12

A friend of mine told me that you're only doing something wrong if you get caught. Is that true?

"As I have observed, those who plow evil and those who sow trouble reap it."

JOB 4:8

I got forced into a fight, but I didn't back off. What can I do next time?

Peacemakers who sow in peace raise a harvest of righteousness.

JAMES 3:18

I feel guilty for not spending time with God. What can I do?

There is no condemnation for those who are in Christ Jesus.

ROMANS 8:1

stand what helps and what hinders friendships.

- **Conflict.** All friendships go through times of conflict. That's a normal part of friendship. Good friends help each other out during tough times. Wading through problems is possible with good friends.
- **Compassion.** Before throwing out simple advice, the first thing friends need to know is that you have compassion. They want to know if you sincerely care about them and that you're willing to share in their struggle. Compassion means "shared pain." You're sharing the pain they feel. If you can be a com-

(There's more!!)

☞

passionate friend, you'll have friends for life.

- **Confrontation.** Confrontation means getting in your friends' face when they need to hear the truth. Many people will want you to tell them what they want to hear. True friends tell you what you need to hear. You demonstrate compassion by helping your friends understand the truth of their situation. Some friends don't want to be confronted for making bad choices. Good friends confront with compassion.
- **Condoning.** When a friend of yours blows it and you say, "Oh, that's okay," but inside you really feel like you should say something, that's called "condoning their behavior." Condoning is the opposite of taking a stand for what you believe to be true. It's letting a friend slide into a lifestyle

(Next page, please.)

☞

I regret thinking that my bad choices wouldn't affect my relationship with God. How can I change my attitude?

Do not be deceived: God cannot be mocked. A man reaps what he sows. The one who sows to please his sinful nature, from that nature will reap destruction; the one who sows to please the Spirit, from the Spirit will reap eternal life.

GALATIANS 6:7–8

Am I really any different than I was before I became a Christian?

Therefore, if anyone is in Christ, he is a new creation; the old has gone, the new has come!

2 CORINTHIANS 5:17

I feel like I take God for granted; will he always forgive me when I blow it?

What shall we say, then? Shall we go on sinning so that grace may increase? By no means! We died to sin; how can we live in it any longer?

ROMANS 6:1–2

Where is God when I struggle between living for him or living for myself?

Do not offer the parts of your body to sin, as instruments of wickedness, but rather offer yourselves to God, as those who have been brought from death to life; and offer the parts of your body to him as instruments of righteousness.

ROMANS 6:13

Why is it so hard for me to choose which path to follow in life?

Living beyond Regret

"Enter through the narrow gate. For wide is the gate and broad is the road that leads to destruction, and many enter through it. But small is the gate and narrow the road that leads to life, and only a few find it."

MATTHEW 7:13–14

Life's Not Fair

Raw Deal #2

Unjust?

I grew up outnumbered. One brother. Five sisters. Life's not fair. Have you ever felt like a pincushion for your sister's fingernails? Did you ever get blamed for beating up your little brother when you never even touched him? Let's face it . . . life's not fair.

Growing up in a large family, I quickly learned that life did not revolve around me. My parents did not try to make life perfect for each of their seven kids. They were more interested in raising a family than in making sure everyone got their fair

---

that could destroy them. Condoning is allowing yourself to lose perspective on what a true friend is. Condoning is saying "yes" when you feel like saying "no." And vice versa. It's a "giving in" type of friendship that avoids confrontation at the cost of what you believe. Condoning weakens friendships.

- **Condemnation.** Condemnation is being judge, jury, and prosecutor. A good friend doesn't condemn. Condemning a friend passes a stiff sentence that can imprison the friendship. What a struggling friend needs most is not condemnation but support. Someone who's wrestling with a problem needs to hear this from you: "If you're willing to work on this problem, I'm going to be here to help and encourage you. And even if you blow off our friendship, I'll still be here waiting for you when you come back." Condemnation kills friendships.
- **Communication.** Talking clears, clarifies, and creates bridges to solving problems. Being a good listener is the first step to effective communication.

(One to go!!)

☞

share. As a screaming brat, I had a hard time understanding this. Now that I'm a father of four children, my parents seem a whole lot wiser. We can be part of God's family and realize that life isn't always going to be fair or we can lie on the kitchen floor, kicking and screaming, "She got more than me! She got more than me! It's not fair!"

The sooner you realize that life is an adventure, the more you can enjoy the ride. When you're on an adventure, the unexpected always happens. Planes are missed, travel plans get messed up, and luggage gets lost. We can either take the adventure as it comes and enjoy each day God gives us or we can fold our arms, put a pout on our face, and say, "This isn't fair." If you do, you'll probably hear the same thing I often heard my parents say: "Tough."

You can tell a good friend not by how much the person talks to you but by how well he or she listens to you. Listening to a friend in trouble will help you understand the person's problem and how you can be of the most help. Most of the time, all a friend needs is someone to listen to them. How many times have you been able to solve your own problem just by talking it out with someone who cared enough to listen? You can be that person!

(That's all!)

What's the incentive for trying to do what's right?

He holds victory in store for the upright, he is a shield to those whose walk is blameless, for he guards the course of the just and protects the way of his faithful ones.

PROVERBS 2:7–8

My youth pastor plays favorites; is that fair?

God does not show favoritism.

ROMANS 2:11

How I can be fair with all my friends?

Life's Not Fair

Then you will understand what is right and just and fair—
every good path. For wisdom will enter your heart, and knowledge will be pleasant to your soul.

PROVERBS 2:9–10

I look at this world and wonder: Is God really just?

What then shall we say? Is God unjust? Not at all!

ROMANS 9:14

My friend and I put in the same amount of time
on a service project, but she got all the praise;
is that fair?

God is not unjust; he will not forget
your work and the love you have
shown him as you have helped his
people and continue to help them.

HEBREWS 6:10

Where is God when I get made fun of for
standing up for him?

For it is commendable if a man bears
up under the pain of unjust suffering
because he is conscious of God. But how
is it to your credit if you receive a beating for
doing wrong and endure it? But if you suffer for
doing good and you endure it, this is commendable
before God.

1 PETER 2:19–20

It seems totally unfair that Jesus had to die for us. Why did he
have to?

He himself bore our sins in his body on the tree, so that we
might die to sins and live for righteousness; by his wounds
you have been healed.

1 PETER 2:24

Why does it seem like I have more struggles than my friends do?

A righteous man may have many troubles, but the LORD delivers him from them all.

PSALM 34:19

My friend accused me of gossiping about her. What can I tell her to make her believe me when I say I didn't?

The mouth of the righteous man utters wisdom, and his tongue speaks what is just.

PSALM 37:30

What qualities does God want me to show to others who've been unfair to me?

Even in darkness light dawns for the upright, for the gracious and compassionate and righteous man.

PSALM 112:4

Getting the Blame

I Didn't Do It

When I was in seventh grade, I got blamed for stealing seventy-five dollars. I had been over at my friend's house when his grandpa told me to leave. I didn't know why he would say such a thing, so I asked him why. "You know why!" he screamed. I didn't know why. "Because you stole the seventy-five dollars that was sitting right on this counter!" Something deep inside my gut felt funny. Something wasn't right. I didn't know what he was talking about. *I didn't steal his money. I didn't even see any money on the counter. Why is he blaming me?* I wondered.

I ran out the door, and he chased me out, telling me never to come back. He followed me into the front yard just as my dad was pulling up in our driveway across the street. Seeing that something was going on, my dad got out of the car and crossed the street. "What's going on here, Joey?" he asked. Those funny feelings in my stomach burst out in tears as I pointed at the old man and cried, "He says I stole his seventy-five dollars. I didn't take any of his money. I didn't do anything!" "That boy isn't welcome in this home until he returns every penny of the money he took," the old man countered. "Pipe down," my dad said to him. "He didn't take your money. He said he didn't, and I believe him." Thanks, Dad.

Getting blamed for something you didn't do produces a gnawing feeling in your stomach. Trying to defend yourself just makes you look guilty if the other person is convinced you did it. To this very day, my dad is a hero to me. He stood up for me even before I had a chance to explain to him what happened. He believed me. He also believed *in* me. He didn't make me try to prove myself. He trusted me when others were accusing me.

When you get nailed for something you didn't do, remember that God is your witness. He saw the whole thing. He'll stand up for you when no one else will. He trusts you when others are accusing you. I hope you have a dad on this earth as great as my dad. If not, your heavenly dad is ready to tell your accusers, "Pipe down."

Bored to Death

I'm confused and I need your help. I live in Southern California, a La-La Land loaded with tons of things to do, and I can't tell you how many times I've heard teenagers say, "I'm bored. There's nothing to do around here."

Where doooo theeese people come from?

I'm out the door, and five minutes later my toes are toasting on warm, soft sand as I check out the waves and wonder if I should surf, swim, or catch sand-crabs. Up the freeway, there's Dizzyland, Knott's Scary Farm, and Tragic Mountain—all with gut-splitting rides to unload my lunch for the price of admission. No cash? I can grab my mountain bike or rock-climbing gear and head to the local mountains for single-track insanity and climbing routes so scary they make Freddy Krueger's teenage sister look attractive. Weekend

(Don't stop!!)
☞

entertainment? A twenty-four-hour megahollywoodopolis 4,374 screen theater just opened nearby. (Okay, it's only a twenty-one-screen theater, but that's still huge!)

When all else fails, there's still TV . . . right?

I don't get it. This place is filled with things to do, but teenagers still claim they get bored. I even know a guy whose punk rock band is named "Bored to Death." He adamantly claims there's nothing to do in this land of sun, surf, and snow. Do this guy and I live on the same planet?

Get back to me quick. If this guy comes over to my house and dies in my living room from boredomticulitis, my mom's gonna be ticked! It drives her crazy when I leave my friends laying around the house.

Desperately yours,
Confused in So Cal

(There's more on page 67.)

☞

I've been accused of not being a Christian because of some bad mistakes I've made. What can I do to change?

Examine yourselves to see whether you are in the faith; test yourselves. Do you not realize that Christ Jesus is in you— unless, of course, you fail the test?

2 CORINTHIANS 13:5

My best friend is mad at me for a fight she started. What can I say to her?

"If your brother sins against you, go and show him his fault, just between the two of you. If he listens to you, you have won your brother over."

MATTHEW 18:15

How should I react when I get in trouble for arguing with my sister but I didn't even start it?

Do everything without complaining or arguing, so that you may become blameless and pure, children of God without fault in a crooked and depraved generation, in which you shine like stars in the universe.

PHILIPPIANS 2:14–15

Getting the Blame

Why should I get blamed for being home late when I couldn't get a ride?

Anyone, then, who knows the good he ought to do and doesn't do it, sins.

JAMES 4:17

The gang I hang out with is always getting in trouble. A few of the guys say they're Christians; how can I tell if they really are?

They claim to know God, but by their actions they deny him.

TITUS 1:16

How should I react when my older brother gets all the attention because he never does anything wrong?

Do not be like Cain, who belonged to the evil one and murdered his brother. And why did he murder him? Because his own actions were evil and his brother's were righteous.

1 JOHN 3:12

I got grounded for cussing. Why should I get grounded if my dad does it too?

We all stumble in many ways. If anyone is never at fault in what he says, he is a perfect man, able to keep his whole body in check.

JAMES 3:2

Self-Pity

Poor Me

 When I'm tempted to complain, I sometimes think about my best friend, Dana, who died a number of years ago of cancer. Dana was a modern-day Job. Job was the guy in the Old Testament who lost his family, livestock, servants, and was inflicted with

huge boils from head to toe. All because he was a righteous man who loved God. Satan wanted Job to curse God, but Job knew better. "His wife said to him, 'Are you still holding on to your integrity? Curse God and die!' He replied, 'You are talking like a foolish woman. Shall we accept good from God, and not trouble?' In all this, Job did not sin in what he said" (Job 2:9–10).

Within four short years, my friend Dana lost his father. The house he grew up in was taken away. He contracted cancer. His family belongings were burnt up by an arsonist. He got shingles all over his body. His truck was stolen. He endured radiation, chemotherapy, and several major operations. He was ripped off by his insurance company, which was subsequently indicted for insurance fraud. If anyone had reason to curse God and whine "Poor me," it was Dana.

Ask anyone who knew Dana, and you would hear about a humble, gentle, warm human being who radiated God's love. Dana could never curse the God he loved and knew so well. He was a paramedic who dreamed of going to foreign countries as a medical missionary. He also served with me as a youth leader for five years. While his health withered away, his smile and caring spirit breathed life. Never once did I hear Dana complain, cursing his circumstances or his God. Do I have much to complain about? I am humbled by Dana. He reminds me of Christ.

Where is God when I feel like I don't have any friends who support me?

If one falls down, his friend can help him up. But pity the man who falls and has no one to help him up!

ECCLESIASTES 4:10

Self-Pity

BORING IN ON BOREDOM

It doesn't matter if you live in La-La Land, the little Hawaiian island of Lanai, Podunkville, or a mile off Toadsuck Road, Arkansas (it's a real place—been there!). It doesn't matter if you're a teenager, a tyrannical two-year-old, or a terribly boring history teacher. You could be a loser, a jock, a beauty queen, a skater, a dweeb, a rocker, a biker, a brain, or just an average student . . . boredom affects everyone. You get bored. I get bored. We all get bored.

Boredom bores (that's digs, tunnels, and drills) into the heart of every human being.

Now if someone has been accused of being boring, that's a problem we don't have time to deal with here. That's what those support groups are for—you know—when everyone sits in a circle and says, "Hi! My name's Ted, and I'm boring."

Boredom, the state of being B-O-R-E-D, not being a dull, pathetically boring person, is what we're talking about. Boredom strikes fear in the hearts of most teenagers. It is the evil triplet sister of those other two teenage terrors: Embarrassment and Caught-In-Public-With-Your-Parents. In fact, research shows that if you're a teenager and you LIKE to be bored, then you really should be examined by a physician to make sure you have a pulse (the same study also concluded that research causes boredom in lab rats).

Though this soggy state of emotional numbness can be nailed right next to that other familiar anthem, "There's nothing to do today," most teenagers don't get bored because of a lack of things to do. Teenagers get bored because of not focusing on the truly important things to do.

READ THE GOOD BOOK

Don't tell me; I already know what you're gonna say: "Whenever I say I'm bored, my mom tells me to read a good book." (This usually only works for moms.) I'm asking you to do two things a bit more radical than reading one of your mom's romance novels.

First, don't read just any book, read *the Book*—the Bible—God's Word. You'll find

(Read on!!)

☞

dozens of ideas for living a life of meaning and significance, which just happens to be the real cure for boredom. I know that doesn't sound as thrilling as seeing the new *Amazonian Piranhas Attack Appomattox* thriller, but that's the problem with overdosing on too much techno-entertainment stuff. Going to Dismalland, er, Disneyland, or Six Flags over Khisbeckizstan is fun . . . for a while. But amusement parks, television, movies, video games, or even catching the perfect wave won't satisfy our deepest desires for living a purpose-filled life. Whether you know it or not, your heart desires something a lot more significant than scoring 10,386,107,100 on Mortal Wombat. Au contraire, God's Word shows us that real meaning and purpose are rooted in a radical love for him. God's Word is the place to discover his love and how to love him. That is what brings true meaning and satisfaction in life.

Second, the best way to blast through boredom is to get your eyes off entertaining

(One to go!!)
☞

My friend put a big dent in my car. How can I keep from being too upset?

Turn my eyes away from worthless things; preserve my life according to your word.

PSALM 119:37

How can I keep my faith when things don't happen as I expect?

Do any of the worthless idols of the nations bring rain? Do the skies themselves send down showers? No, it is you, O LORD our God. Therefore our hope is in you, for you are the one who does all this.

JEREMIAH 14:22

I'm sick of getting picked on by others; where should I turn?

"I call to the LORD, who is worthy of praise, and I am saved from my enemies."

2 SAMUEL 22:4

Why shouldn't I complain when things don't go my way?

"But be sure to fear the LORD and serve him faithfully with all your heart; consider what great things he has done for you."

1 SAMUEL 12:24

Does God really care about my problems?

He will take pity on the weak and the needy and save the needy from death.

PSALM 72:13

Self-Pity

People tell me I need to grow up and stop complaining about my problems. How can I live my life in a better way?

And we pray this in order that you may live a life worthy of the Lord and may please him in every way: bearing fruit in every good work, growing in the knowledge of God.

COLOSSIANS 1:10

What is God's purpose for my going through problems?

"He cuts off every branch in me that bears no fruit, while every branch that does bear fruit he prunes so that it will be even more fruitful."

JOHN 15:2

Questioning God
Hey, God!

 God can handle any question you throw at him; your questions can't intimidate, frighten, startle, or make him feel insecure. Your questions are important to God because he cares about you. He knows that getting a good answer starts with asking an intelligent question. Don't worry about stupid questions either; he gets those all the time. Every question you ask is meaningful to God.

In following God, we'll discover the answers as we go. Some we'll discover sooner. Other answers we'll discover later. When you've got a question on your mind, it's okay to shout, "Hey, God!" to get his attention. Just don't expect him to stand at attention like a new recruit. He's God. He has a bit more seniority than you or I.

Is it okay that I sometimes complain about God's way of doing things?

yourself by beginning to serve others. When you have your heart set on serving your neighbors, kids at school, people at church or in your community, you won't find yourself sitting around on a Saturday picking your ear while groaning the boredom blues. Get a buddy and wash an old person's car—while you're at it, nail your buddy with an explosive jet spray of water to the head. Volunteer at a local soup kitchen or secondhand store for the poor. (You just may find a vintage pair of 70s era pea-green plaid pants!) You don't have to live this life with a chronic case of boredomticulitis. Remember that boredom is primarily an attitude and a choice. God's Word gives you a powerful escape route to a wild life of meaning and purpose through serving others. Give yourself away to others in the name of Jesus and you'll never end up with a tombstone that reads "Bored to Death."

(That's all!)

"Woe to him who quarrels with his Maker, to him who is but a potsherd among the potsherds on the ground. Does the clay say to the potter, 'What are you making?' Does your work say, 'He has no hands'?"

ISAIAH 45:9

Is it okay for me to question God's plans for my life?

The LORD foils the plans of the nations; he thwarts the purposes of the peoples. But the plans of the LORD stand firm forever, the purposes of his heart through all generations.

PSALM 33:10–11

Sometimes I'm afraid to give my plans to God; how can I be sure he'll guide me?

In his heart a man plans his course, but the LORD determines his steps.

PROVERBS 16:9

Is it possible to outsmart God?

There is no wisdom, no insight, no plan that can succeed against the LORD.

PROVERBS 21:30

Does God understand my past and my future?

"I make known the end from the beginning, from ancient times, what is still to come. I say: My purpose will stand, and I will do all that I please."

ISAIAH 46:10

Questioning God

Is it possible to change God's mind if we pray hard enough?

"But he stands alone, and who can oppose him? He does whatever he pleases."

JOB 23:13

Who has ultimate control here on earth—God or man?

All the peoples of the earth are regarded as nothing. He does as he pleases with the powers of heaven and the peoples of the earth. No one can hold back his hand or say to him: "What have you done?"

DANIEL 4:35

How can I be sure that God really created the earth?

"This is what the LORD says—the Holy One of Israel, and its Maker: Concerning things to come, do you question me about my children, or give me orders about the work of my hands? It is I who made the earth and created mankind upon it. My own hands stretched out the heavens; I marshaled their starry hosts."

ISAIAH 45:11–12

Taking Responsibility
Who's to Blame?

Not Me! Have you ever said something like this? "I didn't do it. You're looking at the wrong person. Not me. I wasn't even here. Don't blame me. It's not my fault." Avoiding responsibility. It's simple to push off responsibility and avoid getting involved by blaming, pointing the finger, and expecting others to own up to problems that are really our own. Blaming others is a sign of immaturity. It's being a part of the problem. Taking responsibility for your actions shows courage and maturity that comes from knowing others' feelings are on the line. Taking responsibility is being proactive. An active ingredient to finding a solution.

God's Word tells us to look at our motives and actions. That includes accepting or avoiding responsibility. Not long before King David died, he told his son Solomon, "And you, my son Solomon, acknowledge the God of your father, and serve him with wholehearted devotion and with a willing mind, for the LORD searches every heart and understands every motive behind the thoughts" (1 Chron. 28:9). David wanted to emphasize to Solomon that God knows everything about us. He knows when we blame others and when we own up. He knows if we're looking out for our own interests or the interests of others. Blaming others causes us to grow down. Accepting responsibility helps us grow up.

Where is God when I feel like backing out of a tough situation because I don't want to get blamed for something I didn't do?

Brothers, each man, as responsible to God, should remain in the situation God called him to.

1 CORINTHIANS 7:24

What can I say to people in my youth group who are always taking advantage of each other?

"Do not take advantage of each other, but fear your God. I am the LORD your God."

LEVITICUS 25:17

What is God's purpose in testing me?

"Remember how the LORD your God led you all the way in the desert these forty years, to humble you and to test you in order to know what was in your heart, whether or not you would keep his commands."

DEUTERONOMY 8:2

Where is God when I need help being honest even when I might get in trouble?

"I know, my God, that you test the heart and are pleased with integrity."

1 CHRONICLES 29:17

No one wants to take responsibility for the problems in our youth group; what should we do?

Each one should test his own actions. Then he can take pride in himself, without comparing himself to somebody else.

GALATIANS 6:4

My friend and I can't solve this fight we're in. How can God help us?

Let us examine our ways and test them, and let us return to the LORD.

LAMENTATIONS 3:40

Is it okay to test God?

Jesus answered him, "It is also written: 'Do not put the Lord your God to the test.'"

MATTHEW 4:7

Evil in the World
Why's There So Much Evil?

 Reading the front page is depressing. Today I read about starvation in Africa, gang rape victims in Bosnia-Herzegovina, and neo-Nazi hate crimes in Germany. Why is there so much evil in this world? Why does God allow it? If he's really in control, can't he do something?

Evil in the World   73

What Keeps Me Coming Back to God?

Why should you and I keep following Jesus Christ? With so much evil, suffering, hardship, doubt, and struggle in this world, why should we keep coming back to God every morning to say in one way or another, "Not my will but your will be done"? Why keep asking God, "Why?" Out of all the choices and decisions we have the freedom to make each day, why take a road that is straight, narrow, confusing, challenging, and filled with obstacles? If you've made the decision to be the person God is creating you to be, what keeps you com-

(Keep going!!)
☞

I've been thinking about these questions a lot lately, and I haven't discovered any easy answers. The only thing that makes sense to me is Jesus' dying on a cross for the sin of humankind. I do believe evil exists. I see it all over the place. I see it in others. I see it in myself. In the midst of a world slammed by natural disasters, human suffering, war, and broken families, Jesus is the only one who adequately addresses the problem of human suffering. Jesus confronted evil with his own flesh. He suffered on a cross. He identified himself with human suffering by allowing himself to be touched by it. Pierced by it. Beaten by it. And nailed to a cross by it.

Evil never triumphed over Jesus. Little did Jesus' executioners know, but when Jesus was nailed to the cross, evil was also sentenced to death. Jesus overcame death when he rose to life after being in the tomb for three days. He promises to wipe out all evil when he comes back to redeem this broken world. Evil's been sentenced to death. Evil won't be around much longer. I can hardly wait.

Why are so many intelligent people atheists? How can they be smart and not believe in God?

74   *Evil in the World*

"The wise will be put to shame; they will be dismayed and trapped. Since they have rejected the word of the LORD, what kind of wisdom do they have?"

JEREMIAH 8:9

Why do evil people prosper and good people suffer?

In this meaningless life of mine I have seen both of these: a righteous man perishing in his righteousness, and a wicked man living long in his wickedness.

ECCLESIASTES 7:15

Do wicked people ever pay for their wickedness?

The righteousness of the blameless makes a straight way for them, but the wicked are brought down by their own wickedness.

PROVERBS 11:5

Why do evil people continue to do evil?

Though grace is shown to the wicked, they do not learn righteousness; even in a land of uprightness they go on doing evil and regard not the majesty of the LORD.

ISAIAH 26:10

How am I supposed to make a difference for God in an indifferent world?

"You are the light of the world. A city on a hill cannot be hidden. Neither do people light a lamp and put it under a bowl. Instead they put it on its stand, and it gives light to every-

ing back to him each day? As I think about all the questions I have for God, here's what has kept me coming back to him.

• **Allure.** Out of all the mysteries in this world, none allures me more than the mystery of who God is. Wondering who God is is a daily adventure. Paul the apostle said, "I want to know Christ and the power of his resurrection and the fellowship of sharing in his sufferings, becoming like him in his death" (Phil. 3:10). I don't know about you, but knowing Christ like Paul wanted to know him is going to take me a lifetime. I like what he says, but I'm still trying to figure how to do that. Following Christ is a journey that brings us closer to knowing the God who intimately knows us.

• **Attraction.** Our refrigerator at home is filled with magnets holding up our favorite pictures of family and friends. I call it our "Wall of Fame." Knowing that God passionately loves me draws me to him every day. His love is attractive. It pulls and connects me to him more powerfully than any magnet on our fridge.

(One to go!!)
☞

Evil in the World

75

• **Awe.** God inspires me to be in awe of him; he creates a sense of wonder in me like nothing else in this world. Each morning, he splatters the wakening sky with a paletteful of colors. At the end of every day, he whips out his brushes again and puts on the final touches of red, pink, and orange. His creation throws running deer across my path as I ride my mountain bike through the hills. At a river's edge, two squealing otters pounce on each other, wrestling and chasing each other ten feet from where I sit. Five minutes later, a doe and its fawn appear across the river to drink the cool waters. My God is an *awesome* God. I don't care if that word is overused. It's true.

Allure. Attraction. Awe. These three things keep me coming back to God each day. What keeps you coming back?

(That's all!)

one in the house. In the same way, let your light shine before men, that they may see your good deeds and praise your Father in heaven."

MATTHEW 5:14–16

For you were once darkness, but now you are light in the Lord. Live as children of light.

EPHESIANS 5:8

What should Christians do when they are persecuted for following Jesus?

"But I tell you: Love your enemies and pray for those who persecute you, that you may be sons of your Father in heaven. He causes his sun to rise on the evil and the good, and sends rain on the righteous and the unrighteous."

MATTHEW 5:44–45

How can I really live like a Christian?

Who is wise and understanding among you? Let him show it by his good life, by deeds done in the humility that comes from wisdom.

JAMES 3:13

Has everyone turned away from God?

We all, like sheep, have gone astray, each of us has turned to his own way; and the LORD has laid on him the iniquity of us all.

ISAIAH 53:6

Evil in the World

3

What God Says

Ever get rejected by a guy or girl? I mean, with a slam-dunk, in-your-face, you-are-not-worth-cereal-dust-left-at-the-bottom-of-the-box, you-are-the-nightmare-of-my-waking-day, get-out-of-my-face-out-of-my-way-out-of-my-life, you-do-not-exist-in-my-mind-sight-or-imagination R-E-J-E-C-T-I-O-N? Ouch. Love has never been so lonely.

How does it feel to be passionately . . . madly . . . hopelessly . . . desperately in love with the person of your dreams and know they couldn't care less about you? They refuse to acknowledge your existence. You are little more than a breath of air to them. This person you dream about consumes your thought life. You write them love letters that will never be sent. You lip-sync love songs to them in the mirror. You scribble their name four hundred and eighty-two times on your math notebook. The only time you spend with them is in your dreams . . . wake up! And stop kissing your pillow! In their mind, you do not exist. You are so invisible that they can walk right through you. Dust on the windowsill gets more attention than you. Rejection. What a drag.

God knows what it's like to love someone and get rejected. He loves the whole, entire world, and he gets rejected all the time. How would you like it if you created something that could change the world and your idea got rejected? What if you created an ozone patch kit to prevent the human race from turning into raisins? What if you developed an Oxy-5,000,000 oil-slick degreaser that could clean the ocean? Or what if you designed the world's first non-polluting, trash-burning automobile engine? What if all your ideas and plans could radically redesign the way the world lives but every single one of them got rejected? I think God would understand how you feel. He created the world and every person in it. He has a complete and perfect plan for every human being. But he still gets rejected by people all the time. No matter how good he is or how incredible his ideas are or how much he loves people, people still reject him.

The Bible starts with who God is and what he says. It doesn't start with who we are or what we think. God gave us the Bible to help us discover who he is and how we can get to know him. Human beings are not the most important figures in the Bible ... God *is*. We find out who we are when we find out who God is. When the Bible says that God is the Creator of the heavens and the earth, we discover that we're not just standing on a mound of dirt, we're standing on God's turf. When we read in the Bible that God created man and woman, we can say, "Wow, I'm created by God. I'm part of his design. I'm included in his plan of creation." And as we discover more about what the

What God Says

Bible says who God is and who we are in relation to God, we find out how we can have a relationship, a friendship with God himself.

This chapter will help you understand who God is. And it starts with what he says. If you have a better idea of who God is, you'll find it easier to get to know him. You see, what God says about who he is makes a big difference in how we relate to him. When you read about God's faithfulness, you'll know you have a lifelong friend. When you read about his love, you'll feel comfortable being yourself. And you can bet that when you read about all the other attributes of God, you'll discover how amazing he really is. You will never be the same. Knowing God will help you put your problems in their place. You'll understand that he always hangs out with you. If you've ever been rejected, you'll understand how he feels about rejection. Best of all, you'll learn that he will never reject you. That's what God says.

God's Promises
Creature Comforts

 Plush sofas. Soft pillows. A warm fire. Mellow music floating in the air. Complete relaxation. Ah . . . creature comforts. Living a life of ease and luxury is a fantasy most people dream about but few experience. Cruising through life with ease is a mirage that evaporates when the searing heat of struggle burns through our comfort zones. Comfort zones get torched quicker than they're created. When your comfort zones are going down in flames, where do you go for the cool breeze of comfort?

For thousands of years, people in the midst of pain and hardship have daily gone to God's Word to find the comfort they need. God's Word is filled with thousands of promises to comfort and encourage people no matter what they're facing. When

Ooohh, Now That Looks Tempting

Temptation. Gulp! The word alone puts a lump in our throats. I know of no other explosive subject that will clear a room full of teenagers quicker than a fire drill, bomb scare, or perhaps, a long list of chores to do on the weekend. Temptation is a scary subject. It makes us squirm. Temptation seduces us. It reveals areas of our lives that are anything but strengths. Like a sharp pin piercing a voodoo doll, temptation pricks our consciences with all sorts of guilt, remorse over past mistakes, and nagging doubts of our ability to ever overcome it.

Let's face it: We don't like to talk about our weaknesses. We may have pumped-up pecs from hours in the gym or plenty of mental muscle, but frankly, a lot of us are pretty embarrassed when it comes to the size of our spiritual muscles. Temptation,

(Read on!!)
☞

problems blast open their comfort zones, a lot of young people get ticked off at God: Why did God let this happen to me? If God really loves me, why doesn't he fix this problem now? Hey, God, why me?

God, the God of all comfort, gives you the assurance of his presence every day. He doesn't promise a life of luxury. He promises you his peace and his presence. No creature comfort could ever give you that.

Where is God when I'm having an awful day?

Even though I walk through the valley of the shadow of death, I will fear no evil, for you are with me; your rod and your staff, they comfort me.

PSALM 23:4

Does God really comfort those who are suffering?

But God, who comforts the downcast, comforted us by the coming of Titus.

2 CORINTHIANS 7:6

Will God comfort me with his love whenever I need him?

May your unfailing love be my comfort, according to your promise to your servant.

PSALM 119:76

God's Promises

I made a bunch of serious mistakes because I was angry at God; if I confess, will he forgive me?

"I have seen his ways, but I will heal him; I will guide him and restore comfort to him."

ISAIAH 57:18

Will God comfort me when my heart is weighed down by all sorts of pressures and problems?

"I will turn their mourning into gladness; I will give them comfort and joy instead of sorrow."

JEREMIAH 31:13

Where is God when I am made fun of for being a Christian?

Give me a sign of your goodness, that my enemies may see it and be put to shame, for you, O LORD, have helped me and comforted me.

PSALM 86:17

I'm grieving because my father passed away recently. Will God comfort me?

"Blessed are those who mourn, for they will be comforted."

MATTHEW 5:4

How can I comfort a friend who's disappointed with God?

For you know that we dealt with each of you as a father deals with his own children, encouraging, comforting and urging you to live lives worthy of God, who calls you into his kingdom and glory.

1 THESSALONIANS 2:11–12

God's People

Church Chat

The church is God's people. It isn't a funky, old building or a glass skyscraper reaching to the heavens. The church is a community of people. And people are weird. That means there are going to be weird people in church. God's weird church. The church he loves.

Some people get really hung up about what church should or shouldn't be. According to Scripture, the church is a gathering of fellow sinners. A group of people who admit they are powerless to make any real changes in their lives without God. A bunch of beggars who've found a loaf of bread named Jesus.

What keeps a lot of people out of church is the idea that they have to be perfect or have their life all together to attend. No way. Even though a lot of people talk about others being the "pillars of the church" and "strong Christians," the only "strong" Christians are those who recognize their weaknesses. Weak Christians give control of their lives to God. If you've stayed away from church because of weird people or if you think you're not good enough to go, don't worry. You're invited. There's plenty of room in God's weird and weak church. The one he loves.

Will just going to church get me into heaven?

If you confess with your mouth, "Jesus is Lord," and believe in your heart that God raised him from the dead, you will be saved. For it is with your heart that you believe and are justified, and it is with your mouth that you confess and are saved.

ROMANS 10:9–10

What should I say to the people at my church who are complete hypocrites?

"How can you say to your brother, 'Brother, let me take the speck out of your eye,' when you yourself fail to see the plank in your own eye? You hypocrite, first take the plank out of your eye, and then you will see clearly to remove the speck from your brother's eye."

LUKE 6:42

How can I get my parents to let me go on an inner-city mission trip that all my friends are going on?

Pray in the Spirit on all occasions with all kinds of prayers and requests.

EPHESIANS 6:18

My youth group seems interested only in numbers; how can I get them to be interested in me?

You understand, O LORD; remember me and care for me.

JEREMIAH 15:15

How am I supposed to grow as a Christian when my church doesn't make Christianity relevant to my life?

"And now, O Israel, what does the LORD your God ask of you but to fear the LORD your God, to walk in all his ways, to love him, to serve the LORD your God with all your heart and with all your soul, and to observe the LORD's commands and decrees that I am giving you today for your own good?"

DEUTERONOMY 10:12–13

Some religious people are so phony; how can I keep from becoming like them?

especially when we give in to it, makes us look like spiritual wimps. And nobody wants to look like a wimp.

You see, if we're really honest with one another, we'll be willing to admit that we all struggle with temptation. The difficult part though, the really frustrating part of temptation, is that most of us don't know *how* to talk about temptation. It's embarrassing. At times, downright humiliating. A lot of us feel that if we talk about temptation, others are going to look at us as if we're some sicko-weirdo-stranger-than-strange pervert. So, instead of being honest and supportive of one another as brothers and sisters in Christ, we allow temptation to get us tongue-tied. And we struggle silently.

If you're thinking, "There's got to be a better way; I can't do it alone," you're right . . . there is. Consider this: *Uno* . . . you're not alone in struggling with temptation. You and every other person on this earth face dozens of temptations every single

(Lots more!!)

☞

God's People

Religion that God our Father accepts as pure and faultless is this: to look after orphans and widows in their distress and to keep oneself from being polluted by the world.

JAMES 1:27

I've had a very negative experience with church; what should I do?

See to it, brothers, that none of you has a sinful, unbelieving heart that turns away from the living God. But encourage one another daily, as long as it is called Today, so that none of you may be hardened by sin's deceitfulness.

HEBREWS 3:12–13

Forgiveness
Erasing the Board

 I was never good at math. All the numbers, equations, sines, cosines, formulas, and theoretic postulating never made sense to me. Even worse, I hated getting called up front to solve problems. Walking up to the board, all I could smell was chalkdust and fear. Addition wasn't a problem, but geometry had my head spinning in bisecting trapezoids. Math reminded me of my mistakes. My favorite part of standing at the chalkboard was grabbing the eraser and swiping my incorrect answer into nothingness. My mistakes . . . wiped into eternity.

How many millions of times has your math teacher had to erase the chalkboard? Can your English teachers remember all the Shakespeare quotes they've written on the chalkboard? Can you remember every single mistake you've made on every test you've taken? We tend to forget about the things we hate. God is the same way. When you ask to be forgiven for a mistake you've made, God erases your sin through the blood of his Son, Jesus Christ. He hates sin so much that he'll wipe it away as soon as you ask him. He loves you far more than your mistakes. He

day. *Dos* . . . as a Christian, you need to be equipped and ready for spiritual battle. *Tres* . . . Satan, your spiritual enemy, has a scheme and a strategy for your soul. He will use any trick, lie, or half-truth to trip you up as you follow Jesus. He's got an overcoat of underhanded ways to unravel your resolve to walk with God. Here are just a few.

Lust. Satan has saturated this planet with the seduction that sex will satisfy our every need. Sex on television. Sex in the movies. Sex in the magazines. It's frustrating trying to stay pure in this world. I can't open a favorite surfing magazine without seeing racy ads full of naked, flesh-colored waves . . . and you know I ain't talking about the north shore of Oahu.

Pride. Making ourselves #1 instead of God. Pride comes in all sorts of distorted shapes and sizes. Our clothes. Whether we wear Oakley or Arnette sunglasses. Our attitudes. Our athletic accomplishments. Our brains. Our cars. Our boyfriends or girlfriends.

☞

chucks your sin as far as east is from west. (Try measuring that one!) God loves you so much, he erases your sin. He never counts, multiplies, or divides it. He forgets about the thing he hates most and remembers the person he loves most: you!

What is Jesus' forgiveness all about?

In him we have redemption through his blood, the forgiveness of sins, in accordance with the riches of God's grace.

EPHESIANS 1:7

Does God really want to forgive my sins?

"I will cleanse them from all the sin they have committed against me and will forgive all their sins of rebellion against me."

JEREMIAH 33:8

Am I supposed to forgive others just like God forgives me?

Forgiveness

"For if you forgive men when they sin against you, your heavenly Father will also forgive you. But if you do not forgive men their sins, your Father will not forgive your sins."

MATTHEW 6:14–15

Who really has first place in our lives?

Appetites. What are you hungry for? Food? Acceptance? If you're overweight, food may be your greatest temptation to escape from the pain you're feeling inside. If you're lonely or insecure (is that hard to admit or what?), you may do just about any crazy thing to be accepted by others.

Words. React. Spit back. Attack. The tongue is like a concealed weapon that can be whipped out in a flash. Gossip. Lies. Slander. Cussing. A whole lot of harm can be hurled with two lips and a tongue.

We can learn a lot by what went down in the desert a couple thousand years ago, the place where Jesus was tempted by Satan. Call it a spiritual spring training camp. It's where we can learn how to develop our spiritual muscles against temptation. Open your Bible and read the story of Christ's temptation in Matthew 4:1–11.

Satan attempted to attack Jesus in three distinct ways. First,

(There's more!!)
☞

Does God remember our sins?

"For I will forgive their wickedness and will remember their sins no more."

HEBREWS 8:12

Should I be afraid to ask God for forgiveness?

If we confess our sins, he is faithful and just and will forgive us our sins and purify us from all unrighteousness.

1 JOHN 1:9

What should I do when I feel like hiding my sin?

Then I acknowledged my sin to you and did not cover up my iniquity. I said, "I will confess my transgressions to the LORD"—and you forgave the guilt of my sin.

PSALM 32:5

Does God forgive all my sins or just a few?

You forgave the iniquity of your people and covered all their sins.

PSALM 85:2

Forgiveness

Can I turn to God any time for forgiveness?

Let the wicked forsake his way and the evil man his thoughts. Let him turn to the LORD, and he will have mercy on him, and to our God, for he will freely pardon.

ISAIAH 55:7

Life and Death

Eternity Matters

Ever since I was a little kid, I've had death all around me. My dad is a mortician. An undertaker. He buries people for a living and helps grieving families. Try explaining that one during Show and Tell. You could say my dad works in God's shipping department. If my mom was an obstetrician, we'd also have a receiving department, but since she's not a baby doctor, we only do shipping.

Have you ever considered how long eternity is? There's a big gap between earthly life and eternal life. Eternity matters. If I knew that I was going to be going somewhere longer than the average vacation, I'd want to be prepared. Well prepared.

knowing Jesus hadn't munched on any Powerbars or sipped any Gatorade in over forty days, Satan appealed to Jesus' appetites: "Hey, Jesus, if you're really God's Son, turn these boulders into bagels." Second, Satan tried to get Jesus to seek his approval. He wanted Jesus to prove himself: "If you're really the Son of God, then do a swan dive off this temple. You've got angels to catch you, don't you?" Last, Satan attempted to get Jesus' total life attention, his worship, by offering him the whole world: "Here's the pink slip for

(Don't stop now!!)

☞

Eternity is a fascinating subject. Young people have all sorts of questions about death, life after death, eternity, heaven, and hell. The Bible has loads to say about life after death. The reason Jesus Christ came to earth was so we could spend eternity

Life and Death

planet earth. Worship me and it's all yours."

Though Satan does have a scheme and a strategy to sink your spiritual life, he is not very creative. The same tricks he played on Jesus are the same ones he will use on you. He appeals to your appetites—those desires and yearnings for satisfaction and fulfillment in this life. He will make you try to prove yourself by telling you that your faith is not authentic. He will ask for your attention, your worship, by dazzling you with everything this world has to offer. Tantalizing temptations like wealth, worldly wisdom . . . maybe even a shot or two of whiskey. Anything to get your eyes off God.

Check out how Jesus gets in Satan's face in this story. For every sizzling temptation Satan served him, Jesus backhanded that snake with a sharp blow from the powerful sword of God's Word (see Ephesians 6:17). In every temptation, Jesus had a choice. Follow God or follow Satan. Satan wanted him to think he had no choices. No options. No alternatives. No way out. Satan does the exact same thing with you.

Now read 1 Corinthians 10:13. With Jesus, you always have a way out by having the power of the Holy Spirit in your life. With

(One to go!!)

☞

with his Father. The Bible says that God has set eternity in the hearts of men (Eccles. 3:11) and, without a personal relationship with him, we will be forever separated from him. That's a long time. In Christ Jesus, God promises that eternity is worth getting prepared for. To be unprepared for eternity is like dressing for a party you don't plan on going to. Not preparing for eternity is wasted living. Knowing someone in shipping isn't good enough.

How can I be sure that Jesus is the way to get to heaven?

Jesus answered, "I am the way and the truth and the life. No one comes to the Father except through me."

JOHN 14:6

"I tell you the truth, whoever hears my word and believes him who sent me has eternal life and will not be condemned; he has crossed over from death to life."

JOHN 5:24

I'm scared; how can I be sure that death isn't final?

When the perishable has been clothed with the imperishable, and the mortal with immortality, then the saying that is written will come true: "Death has been swallowed up in victory." "Where, O death, is your victory? Where, O death, is your sting?" The

Life and Death

sting of death is sin, and the power of sin is the law. But thanks be to God! He gives us the victory through our Lord Jesus Christ.

1 CORINTHIANS 15:54–57

Will God welcome me into heaven?

"In my Father's house are many rooms; if it were not so, I would have told you. I am going there to prepare a place for you. And if I go and prepare a place for you, I will come back and take you to be with me that you also may be where I am."

JOHN 14:2–3

Has God included me in his plans for heaven?

"For I know the plans I have for you," declares the LORD, "plans to prosper you and not to harm you, plans to give you hope and a future."

JEREMIAH 29:11

What will heaven be like?

I saw the Holy City, the new Jerusalem, coming down out of heaven from God, prepared as a bride beautifully dressed for her husband. And I heard a loud voice from the throne saying, "Now the dwelling of God is with men, and he will live with them. They will be his people, and God himself will be with them and be their God. He will wipe every tear from their eyes. There will be no more death or mourning or crying or pain, for the old order of things has passed away."

REVELATION 21:2–4

Christian friends, you have a way out by being honest and supporting one another through prayer and accountability. With your youth pastor, you have a way out by receiving ongoing counsel in handling temptation. With an older Christian adult you trust, you have a way out by asking them how they dealt with certain temptations. Satan would love to single you out, isolate you from others, and make you feel like no one else has ever experienced the temptations that tug you down. Temptation can be tiring, but God is faithful. He won't let you be tempted beyond what you can bear. Remember: You stand on grace, the free gift of forgiveness and freedom in Christ. Because of Jesus, you are a child of God and not a slave to sin or temptation. And that's definitely worth talking about.

(That's all!)

How am I supposed to have my mind on eternity when I get so distracted by things on earth?

So we fix our eyes not on what is seen, but on what is unseen. For what is seen is temporary, but what is unseen is eternal.

2 CORINTHIANS 4:18

Is it important to believe in Christ's resurrection or not?

If there is no resurrection of the dead, then not even Christ has been raised. And if Christ has not been raised, our preaching is useless and so is your faith.

1 CORINTHIANS 15:13–14

Does God want everyone to have a relationship with Jesus Christ?

"For my Father's will is that everyone who looks to the Son and believes in him shall have eternal life, and I will raise him up at the last day."

JOHN 6:40

Is eternal life found in Jesus Christ?

We know also that the Son of God has come and has given us understanding, so that we may know him who is true. And we are in him who is true—even in his Son Jesus Christ. He is the true God and eternal life.

1 JOHN 5:20

Counting on Jesus

Faithful Friend

What friend of yours will hang on every word you speak and never cut in with poor advice? What friend of yours isn't a flake? What friend of yours can you count on all the time, no matter what? What friend of yours . . . is completely trustworthy? Will never gossip about you? Believes in you even when you don't believe in yourself? Makes you laugh when you feel like crying? Hangs out with you whenever you want? Likes the things that you like? Picks you first when choosing teams? Calls you every day? Doesn't make you do only what he wants to do? Always says the right thing at the right time? Helps you out when everyone else has abandoned you?

And what friend of yours . . . hopes for the very best in all you do? Smiles at you when everyone else is frowning? Loves you for who you are? Writes you love letters? Wakes you with the morning sun? Closes your day with a beautiful sunset? Flings stars in the heavens to sparkle in your eyes? Applauds for you louder than anyone else? Paints rainbows to remind you of a promise? Creates mountains for you to climb? Will never leave you or forsake you? Provides everything you could possibly need? Helps you out in struggles? Sees your good qualities? Gives you a way out when you're tempted? Is faithful to you even when you're not faithful to him? Loves you more than anybody could or ever will? Would trade his life for yours?

Have you ever had such a faithful friend like Jesus?

Is God faithful even when I'm not?

If we are faithless, he will remain faithful, for he cannot disown himself.

2 TIMOTHY 2:13

Do you have a favorite playground? I do. My favorite place to play is the "mother of all sandboxes." It's filled with rocks, boulders, mountains, and other body-smashing types of quartz monzonite (the actual type of rock found in my playground). My playground is not actually mine; it's owned by the U.S. Government, which has it on loan from God. This playground is a phenomenal chunk of the Southern California desert called Joshua Tree National Monument. Joshua Tree has such an unbelievable amount of rocks, it's as if God grabbed Mt. Everest, crumbled it into bits, and threw it like a fistful of gravel over the high desert. The

(Good stuff, huh! Read on!!)

☞

monument is popular for rich blue skies, golden sunsets, wildflowers, and the very spiny, spindly Joshua Tree. (WARNING: Never sit on a Joshua Tree!)

J. T. is the place where I like to challenge teenagers to do two things: (1) rock climb with ropes, harnesses, and equipment, and (2) be solo with God. The first challenge deals with acrophobia, the fear of heights. We do that by putting about sixty feet of air between each student and the ground, assuring them that it's the landing, not the fall, that hurts. As scary as the first challenge sounds, rock climbing is like walking on the sidewalk compared to challenge #2. The second challenge is being by yourself. Solo. Alone-a-phobia. For at least an hour. Maybe two. Without your friends. No walkman. No MTV. No noise. Just you, God, rocks, and your thoughts.

A solo is a one-on-one time with you and God. You may be by yourself, but you're not alone. You're with your Creator. Most students, even most adults, know *muy poco* about what it means to be alone with God. Solo gives you a chance to learn three very important things:

- **Solitude.** Being by ourselves causes us to look at who we really are. Scary thought! God wants to meet us during those alone times to give us his grace to face our weaknesses through his strength.
- **Silence.** God created the world in silence. We tend to live very noisy lives. Silence helps us to hear God's voice by quieting all the other distractions in our lives. God whispers louder than he shouts.
- **Surrender.** Sitting back in a harness over a hundred-foot cliff is a whole lot easier than saying each day, "Okay, God, I surrender. I give up. You're in control now. I trust you with my life." Total surrender. It's roping up with God, knowing that climbing without a rope is for fools and dead people.

Before Jesus started his public ministry, he went into the desert for a forty-day solo. He wanted to be alone with his Father, but he didn't head for Palm Springs— buzzards doing flybys; frying hot sand; cheap

(One to go!!)

☞

Counting on Jesus

I break commitments all the time; does God ever break his commitments?

He is the Rock, his works are perfect, and all his ways are just. A faithful God who does no wrong, upright and just is he.

DEUTERONOMY 32:4

If I'm faithful to God, will he be faithful to me?

"To the faithful you show yourself faithful, to the blameless you show yourself blameless."

2 SAMUEL 22:26

Is God faithful in everything he does?

For the word of the LORD is right and true; he is faithful in all he does.

PSALM 33:4

I don't know anyone who keeps all their promises. Does God?

The LORD is faithful to all his promises and loving toward all he has made.

PSALM 145:13

Will God keep me walking with him?

May God himself, the God of peace, sanctify you through and through. May your whole spirit, soul and body be kept blameless at the coming of our Lord Jesus Christ. The one who calls you is faithful and he will do it.

1 THESSALONIANS 5:23–24

How faithful a friend is God?

Your love, O LORD, reaches to the heavens, your faithfulness to the skies.

PSALM 36:5

God's Love
Sending the Message

It's for You. You've seen it written all over the place. Spray painted on walls. Printed on bumper stickers. Written across the sky. On tattoos; freeway overpasses; T-shirts; Monday night football; jewelry; billboards; notebooks. Everywhere: God is love.

People are trying to get the message out any way they can. Trying to spread the good news of Jesus Christ has gone to extreme measures. Maybe too extreme. The most effective way to tell others about God's unconditional love is to have it written on your heart. If his love is on your heart, others will never miss it. When God sent Jesus Christ into this lost and hurting world, he wanted his message to be unavoidably distinctive. Changed lives communicate God's love loud and clear. Your life is a message of God's love to each person you meet. He wants to use you to help others experience his grace, acceptance, and love. People need to hear God's message. Give them his love with your changed life. You'll never need to buy spray paint.

What is love?

This is love: not that we loved God, but that he loved us and sent his Son as an atoning sacrifice for our sins.

1 JOHN 4:10

Will God always love me even when I fail to love him?

Then I said: "O LORD, God of heaven, the great and awesome God, who keeps his covenant of love with those who love him and obey his commands. . . ."

NEHEMIAH 1:5

How can I experience God's unconditional love and forgiveness?

God's Love

Have mercy on me, O God, according to your unfailing love; according to your great compassion blot out my transgressions.

PSALM 51:1

Does God ever hold back his love from me?

Praise be to God, who has not rejected my prayer or withheld his love from me!

PSALM 66:20

Can God's love calm me down when I'm stressed out?

"The LORD your God is with you, he is mighty to save. He will take great delight in you, he will quiet you with his love, he will rejoice over you with singing."

ZEPHANIAH 3:17

How did God prove his love for me?

But God demonstrates his own love for us in this: While we were still sinners, Christ died for us.

ROMANS 5:8

leather sandals; mirages sent by Satan himself. There wasn't a watercooler or fridge in sight. Nada. Maybe Jesus was trying to teach us something by spending solo time in the desert with God? You and I will probably never spend forty days alone with God in the desert like Jesus did. (How would you explain that one to the Attendance Office?) But you can start today by having a solo time with your Creator. He's crazy about spending time with you. A few minutes. Half an hour. A few hours? Solitude. Silence. Surrender. Solo helps get your life in order. Solo double-checks to make sure you've got your rope on tight. Solo gets you climbing with God.

(That's all!)

Sometimes I feel empty; how can I be assured of God's love?

But if anyone obeys his word, God's love is truly made complete in him.

1 JOHN 2:5

Can anything separate me from God's love?

Who shall separate us from the love of Christ? Shall trouble or hardship or persecution or famine or nakedness or danger or sword? As it is written: "For your sake we face death all day long; we are considered as sheep to be slaughtered." No,

God's Love

in all these things we are more than conquerors through him who loved us. For I am convinced that neither death nor life, neither angels nor demons, neither the present nor the future, nor any powers, neither height nor depth, nor anything else in all creation, will be able to separate us from the love of God that is in Christ Jesus our Lord.

ROMANS 8:35–39

How can I learn more about God's love for me?

Know therefore that the LORD your God is God; he is the faithful God, keeping his covenant of love to a thousand generations of those who love him and keep his commands.

DEUTERONOMY 7:9

God's Word

Blueprint for Life

One of a Kind. I called my friend Trevor one day and asked him what he was doing. "Oh, just spending some time in the blueprint," he replied. Trevor was studying architecture, but I knew he wasn't in the middle of any project, so I said, "Blueprint? What are you talking about?" I should have guessed. Trevor said, "The Bible. I'm studying the blueprint for life." Duh.

Just like Trevor, God's into architecture and design. Trevor's good at what he does, but God's a lot better. His Word is the complete blueprint you need for your life. God is the master architect, and he has an original design for your life. His Word tells you how to build a foundation. He tells you how to construct a solid life to battle the fiercest of storms. The Bible tells you what to put in your house and what to keep out. Every construction truth and principle you need is in God's blueprint. How much do these plans cost? Nothing. God's plan for your life is free. Absolutely free. The only thing you need to be able to use

God's Word

God's blueprint is a personal relationship with Christ. Without Jesus, God's plan doesn't make much sense. God's plan doesn't lay out decisions for you. He leaves those up to you. He won't tell you what class to pick, who to date on Friday night, or what college to choose for your future. He shows you how to build a life worth living in Christ. His Spirit gives you wisdom and strength to make good decisions, but he leaves the actual work up to you. Check out God's blueprint for your life. He has a perfect plan designed just for you.

I'm eager to learn more about the Bible, but where should I start?

My son, if you accept my words and store up my commands within you, turning your ear to wisdom and applying your heart to understanding, and if you call out for insight and cry aloud for understanding, and if you look for it as for silver and search for it as for hidden treasure, then you will understand the fear of the LORD and find the knowledge of God.

PROVERBS 2:1–5

What can the Bible do in my life?

For the word of God is living and active. Sharper than any double-edged sword, it penetrates even to dividing soul and spirit, joints and marrow; it judges the thoughts and attitudes of the heart.

HEBREWS 4:12

How can I be sure everything the Bible says is true?

For this is what the LORD says—he who created the heavens, he is God; he who fashioned and made the earth, he founded it; he did not create it to be empty, but formed it to

God's Word

Worship the Best or Die like the Rest

COOL WORSHIP IDEAS FOR DIGGING GOD

Feel like you're in a mud-oozing rut with God? Bored with a church that seems totally out of touch for where you're at? Feeling apathetic about this Christianity stuff, wondering if it really makes a difference in your life? Depressed by the desperate dive in your lack of spiritual passion? Finding a tremendous lack of thankfulness in your day-to-day living? Need some time to get away and clear your head, your heart, your life?

Press on, amigo, your feelings will come and go; why eventually die like the rest when you can worship the best? Here's some cool ideas to get the fire back

(More on page 100.)

be inhabited—he says: "I am the LORD, and there is no other. I have not spoken in secret, from somewhere in a land of darkness; I have not said to Jacob's descendants, 'Seek me in vain.' I, the LORD, speak the truth; I declare what is right."

ISAIAH 45:18–19

I get bored reading the Bible; how can I see things in a fresh perspective?

Open my eyes that I may see wonderful things in your law.

PSALM 119:18

Is God's Word relevant to every area of my life?

"Every word of God is flawless; he is a shield to those who take refuge in him."

PROVERBS 30:5

Will God show me how to read the Bible?

Show me your ways, O LORD, teach me your paths; guide me in your truth and teach me, for you are God my Savior, and my hope is in you all day long. Remember, O LORD, your great mercy and love, for they are from of old. Remember not the sins of my youth and my rebellious ways;

God's Word

according to your love remember me, for you are good, O
LORD. Good and upright is the LORD; therefore he instructs sinners in his ways.

PSALM 25:4–8

Will God's Word teach me the difference between right and wrong?

Teach me, O LORD, to follow your decrees; then I will keep
them to the end. Give me understanding, and I will keep your
law and obey it with all my heart.

PSALM 119:33–34

God's Goodness
Good Enough

Thank You!

Raising a two-year-old to be a good little girl
was a fun, chaotic adventure. A creative, curious
heat wave of energy, Janae's personality was
tough to harness. One of her passions
was exploring and playing with anything
that could cause bodily harm. *Janae, put
down that knife. Janae, get away from
the light socket. Janae, take the keys
out of the ignition.* Life with Janae
was never dull. Her curiosity pro-
pelled her into every day with enthu-
siasm and wonder. Sometimes though,
she wanted to be the captain of her own
ship, setting her own course with her three
favorite words "No," "Why," and "Mine." When
she began to write her own version of *Mutiny on the Bounty*
and jumped ship, Mommy and Daddy would look at each other
and say, "I think she needs a 'time out.'" Just like all two-year-

olds, Janae was a good little girl. Sometimes. Just like her daddy.

What would this universe be like if someone had to teach God how to be good? *God, do I need to give you a spanking? God, did you rearrange the planets when I told you not to? God, who taught you that word?* Fortunately, you or I don't have to spend our lives teaching God to be good. He already is. The Bible is filled with verses that talk about the goodness of God. God never learned to be good. He never went to any "God Obedience" classes. God is good. His character is good, always has been good and always will be good. You and I and Janae, we have to learn about goodness through the magnifying lens of our mistakes. We're all like little kids discovering God's goodness. In Christ, we're learning to be good. Not on our own power but on his. That's good.

Will God's goodness carry me through my struggles?

His divine power has given us everything we need for life and godliness through our knowledge of him who called us by his own glory and goodness.

2 PETER 1:3

I am still confident of this: I will see the goodness of the LORD in the land of the living.

PSALM 27:13

---

into your faith and your focus on God.

Time-out trek. Go hiking in the mountains with a friend.

Journal dumping. Start a personal journal. Dump out your prayers, thoughts, and feelings. Be honest with God.

Personal psalm. Read a few psalms in the Bible and then write out your own psalm to God.

Future destination. Visit a graveyard. Spend some time thinking about your future.

Health care. Go to a children's cancer ward. Thank God for your health.

Rock out. Grab your guitar, bongo drums, or kazoo. Create a cool worship song.

Go 5-10-15. Practice being silent before God for five, ten, or fifteen minutes at a time.

Cash giveaway. Worship God with your wallet; give money to someone who can't repay you.

Team effort. Get three or four friends together and create a special worship service for your youth group.

(Don't miss this!)

☞

God's Goodness

Can I experience God's goodness simply by trusting in him?

How great is your goodness, which you have stored up for those who fear you, which you bestow in the sight of men on those who take refuge in you.

PSALM 31:19

Body buildup. Have a candlelight service with singing and Scripture reading.

Do as the Romans. Read Romans 12:1–3. Write out specific ways to live your whole life in worship to God.

(That's all!)

🤚

How will God prove his goodness to me?

And the LORD said, "I will cause all my goodness to pass in front of you, and I will proclaim my name, the LORD, in your presence. I will have mercy on whom I will have mercy, and I will have compassion on whom I will have compassion."

EXODUS 33:19

Will God's goodness always be with me?

Surely goodness and love will follow me all the days of my life, and I will dwell in the house of the LORD forever.

PSALM 23:6

Praise the LORD. Give thanks to the LORD, for he is good; his love endures forever.

PSALM 106:1

Where is God when I need him to answer my prayers?

Answer me, O LORD, out of the goodness of your love; in your great mercy turn to me.

PSALM 69:16

I feel like I'm not a very good Christian; how can I keep from getting discouraged?

He who began a good work in you will carry it on to completion until the day of Christ Jesus.

PHILIPPIANS 1:6

God's Goodness

Is God good to people who feel imprisoned?

Set me free from my prison, that I may praise your name. Then the righteous will gather about me because of your goodness to me.

PSALM 142:7

God's Presence

Side by Side

When I was a junior in college, I studied in Spain for three months. Not only did I learn some *español*, I also got a quick education in the art of being robbed at knifepoint. Sitting in a park one Saturday afternoon, I was minding my own business writing postcards home. From the corner of my eye, I saw two guys quickly approach me and before I knew it they were sitting at my side holding two long, sharp, blood-producing knives. One at my heart. The other at my gut. They scrounged through my knapsack, took my watch (Imitation Casio), and ruffled through my wallet, which only had a dollar in it. *(No dinero, hombre . . . Olé!)*

As they were going through my stuff, I was reflecting on what a drag it was to have lived such a short life and how difficult it was going to be to ship my body back to the States. I thought to myself, "Those knives are going to hurt. Now I know why I always wanted to die in my sleep."

Actually, what I was really doing was praying. Praying hard and fast. *Lord, please, please, please don't let them stick those things in me. Please, God, please, please, please!* In the midst of getting the snot scared out of me, a sudden peace zoomed through me. Kinda like an airplane breaking through turbulence after it passes through a big cloud. Whoosh! I really felt the presence of Christ with me. Side by side. It wasn't as if everything was fine and birds began to sing love songs, but I

Was he just a historical figure like Michelangelo? Was he some sort of magician? Did he really do miracles like people say he did? Is this guy Jesus for real? Who does he say he is? Who does the Bible say he is?

Knowing who Jesus is isn't a matter of *was*. Jesus *is*. He exists today. And yesterday. And *mañana*. You may be wondering who Jesus is and why he's such an important person in history. The Bible, God's love letter to you, is *his-story: the story of Jesus*. Here are just a few verses that will tell you who Jesus is and who the Bible says he is. Make history. Make Jesus the center of your life story.

JESUS IS FIRST AND LAST, THE BEGINNING AND THE END.

"I am the Alpha and the Omega, the First and the Last, the Beginning and the End."

REVELATION 22:13

JESUS IS THE SON OF GOD.

They all asked, "Are you then the Son of God?" He replied, "You are right in saying I am."

LUKE 22:70

JESUS IS THE SON OF MAN.

But Jesus remained silent and gave no answer. Again the high priest asked him, "Are you the Christ, the Son of the Blessed One?" "I am," said Jesus. "And you will see the Son of Man sitting at the right hand of the Mighty One and coming on the clouds of heaven."

MARK 14:61–62

JESUS IS THE MESSIAH.

The woman said, "I know that Messiah" (called Christ) "is coming. When he comes, he will explain everything to us." Then Jesus declared, "I who speak to you am he."

JOHN 4:25–26

JESUS IS THE CHRIST.

"But what about you?" he asked. "Who do you say I am?" Peter answered, "You are the Christ."

MARK 8:29

(Read on!!)

JESUS IS THE HOLY ONE OF GOD.

"Ha! What do you want with us, Jesus of Nazareth? Have you come to destroy us? I know who you are—the Holy One of God!"

LUKE 4:34

JESUS IS THE WORD OF GOD.

The Word became flesh and made his dwelling among us. We have seen his glory, the glory of the One and Only, who came from the Father, full of grace and truth.

JOHN 1:14

JESUS IS THE LAMB OF GOD.

The next day John saw Jesus coming toward him and said, "Look, the Lamb of God, who takes away the sin of the world!"

JOHN 1:29

JESUS IS LORD.

If you confess with your mouth, "Jesus is Lord," and believe in your heart that God raised him from the dead, you will be saved.

ROMANS 10:9

JESUS IS OUR SAVIOR.

"Today in the town of David a Savior has been born to you; he is Christ the Lord."

LUKE 2:11

JESUS IS OUR TEACHER.

"You call me 'Teacher' and 'Lord,' and rightly so, for that is what I am."

JOHN 13:13

JESUS IS THE ROOT AND OFFSPRING OF DAVID, THE BRIGHT MORNING STAR.

"I, Jesus, have sent my angel to give you this testimony for the churches. I am the Root and the Offspring of David, and the bright Morning Star."

REVELATION 22:16

JESUS IS THE TRUE GOD AND ETERNAL LIFE.

We know also that the Son of God has come and has given us understanding, so that we may know him who is true. And we are in him who is true—even in his Son Jesus Christ. He is the true God and eternal life.

1 JOHN 5:20

(There's more!!)

☞

God's Presence

sensed God's Spirit letting me know that he was with me. The robbers finished going through my bag and split as quickly as they came. I wish they would have taken my pocket Bible. They could have used it.

You don't have to get held up to know that Jesus is always with you. He promises to never leave your side. He is always with you. Side by side.

Should I tell others about God's presence in my life?

But as for me, it is good to be near God. I have made the Sovereign LORD my refuge; I will tell of all your deeds.

PSALM 73:28

It seems that I'm the only Christian at my school; what can I do?

"So do not fear, for I am with you; do not be dismayed, for I am your God. I will strengthen you and help you; I will uphold you with my righteous right hand."

ISAIAH 41:10

Is Jesus with me when I feel alone in the midst of a crowd?

"And surely I am with you always, to the very end of the age."

MATTHEW 28:20

Can God's presence in my life make me stronger?

May he strengthen your hearts so that you will be blameless and holy in the presence of our God and Father when our Lord Jesus comes with all his holy ones.

1 THESSALONIANS 3:13

I wonder, can someone as insignificant as me ever get close to God?

Even the sparrow has found a home, and the swallow a nest for herself, where she may have her young—a place near your altar, O Lord Almighty, my King and my God.

PSALM 84:3

Will God forgive me for ignoring him sometimes?

Let us draw near to God with a sincere heart in full assurance of faith, having our hearts sprinkled to cleanse us from a guilty conscience and having our bodies washed with pure water.

HEBREWS 10:22

Where is God when I have to move away from all my Christian friends?

"I am with you and will watch over you wherever you go."

GENESIS 28:15

Where is God when I don't feel his presence in my life?

"The Lord himself goes before you and will be with you; he will never leave you nor forsake you. Do not be afraid; do not be discouraged."

DEUTERONOMY 31:8

Persisting in Prayer
Talking to God

Just Ask. Writing a book takes a long time. Writing a book takes even longer if you're trying to look up hundreds of Bible verses. My friend Jake is a climbing fanatic. He calls me at least two or three times a week to go climbing. For the past two months, I've turned him down. "Sorry, Jake, I've got to write." Every time I see him at

JESUS IS THE WAY, THE TRUTH, AND THE LIFE.

Jesus answered, "I am the way and the truth and the life. No one comes to the Father except through me."

JOHN 14:6

JESUS IS THE TRUE VINE.

"I am the true vine, and my Father is the gardener."

JOHN 15:1

JESUS IS THE LIGHT OF THE WORLD.

"While I am in the world, I am the light of the world."

JOHN 9:5

JESUS IS THE GOOD SHEPHERD.

"I am the good shepherd; I know my sheep and my sheep know me."

JOHN 10:14

JESUS IS THE GATE FOR HIS SHEEP.

Therefore Jesus said again, "I tell you the truth, I am the gate for the sheep."

JOHN 10:7

JESUS IS THE RESURRECTION AND THE LIFE.

Jesus said to her, "I am the resurrection and the life. He who believes in me will live, even though he dies."

JOHN 11:25

JESUS IS OUR GREAT HIGH PRIEST.

Therefore, since we have a great high priest who has gone through the heavens, Jesus the Son of God, let us hold firmly to the faith we profess.

HEBREWS 4:14

JESUS IS THE BREAD OF LIFE.

Then Jesus declared, "I am the bread of life. He who comes to me will never go hungry, and he who believes in me will never be thirsty."

JOHN 6:35

JESUS IS NOT OF "THIS WORLD."

But he continued, "You are from below; I am from above. You are of this world; I am not of this world."

JOHN 8:23

(One to go!!)

☞

Jesus is gentle and humble.

"Take my yoke upon you and learn from me, for I am gentle and humble in heart, and you will find rest for your souls."

MATTHEW 11:29

Jesus is the Righteous One.

My dear children, I write this to you so that you will not sin. But if anybody does sin, we have one who speaks to the Father in our defense—Jesus Christ, the Righteous One.

1 JOHN 2:1

Jesus is the great "I am." (That means "past, present, and future." He's always existed.)

"I tell you the truth," Jesus answered, "before Abraham was born, I am!"

JOHN 8:58

Jesus is the Almighty.

"I am the Alpha and the Omega," says the Lord God, "who is, and who was, and who is to come, the Almighty."

REVELATION 1:8

Jesus is the Living One.

"I am the Living One; I was dead, and behold I am alive for ever and ever! And I hold the keys of death and Hades."

REVELATION 1:18

Jesus is the One who searches hearts and minds.

"Then all the churches will know that I am he who searches hearts and minds, and I will repay each of you according to your deeds."

REVELATION 2:23

Jesus never changes.

Jesus Christ is the same yesterday and today and forever.

HEBREWS 13:8

Jesus is coming soon.

He who testifies to these things says, "Yes, I am coming soon." Amen. Come, Lord Jesus.

REVELATION 22:20

(That's all!)

Persisting in Prayer

church he says the same thing, "When are we going climbing? Have you finished that stupid book yet?" What I like about Jake is that he's persistent. He never gives up. That's what it takes to become a good climber. Persistence is also what it takes to talk to God.

When Jesus spoke about talking to God, he said, "Ask and it will be given to you; seek and you will find; knock and the door will be opened to you. For everyone who asks receives; he who seeks finds; and to him who knocks, the door will be opened. Which of you, if his son asks for bread, will give him a stone? Or if he asks for a fish, will give him a snake?" (Matt. 7:7-10). Prayer is a matter of persistence. Jesus promises that every time you talk with God, your prayers are being heard. God is eager to talk with you. Most of us are really good at asking God for things but not very good at seeking and knocking. Persistence is nonstop seeking and knocking. Persistence means praying when you don't feel like it. Persistence is hanging in there instead of hanging up. Persistence in talking to God is like climbing a rock, searching for the next handhold. You may not be able to see it, but if you keep searching, one appears where you least expect it. God isn't too busy for you. As with any friendship, you need to make a deliberate effort to talk with your friend. Be persistent. Keep seeking. Keep knocking. Keep talking to God. Be like Jake. Keep calling.

I wonder, does God really hear my prayers?

Persisting in Prayer   109

The LORD is far from the wicked but he hears the prayer of the righteous.

PROVERBS 15:29

Should I feel guilty asking God to help me?

The LORD is good, a refuge in times of trouble. He cares for those who trust in him.

NAHUM 1:7

How did Jesus teach his disciples to pray?

"This, then, is how you should pray: 'Our Father in heaven, hallowed be your name, your kingdom come, your will be done on earth as it is in heaven. Give us today our daily bread. Forgive us our debts, as we also have forgiven our debtors. And lead us not into temptation, but deliver us from the evil one.'"

MATTHEW 6:9–13

What does the Bible say about the power of prayer?

The prayer of a righteous man is powerful and effective.

JAMES 5:16

It seems I'm either praying a lot or not at all. How can I be more consistent?

Be joyful in hope, patient in affliction, faithful in prayer.

ROMANS 12:12

I'm afraid to pray out loud. Do I have to?

"But when you pray, go into your room, close the door and pray to your Father, who is unseen. Then your Father, who sees what is done in secret, will reward you."

MATTHEW 6:6

Persisting in Prayer

I don't understand; why do people say "In Jesus' name" when they end a prayer?

"You did not choose me, but I chose you and appointed you to go and bear fruit—fruit that will last. Then the Father will give you whatever you ask in my name."

JOHN 15:16

How often should I pray?

Pray continually.

1 THESSALONIANS 5:17

Did Jesus ever pray?

One of those days Jesus went out to a mountainside to pray, and spent the night praying to God.

LUKE 6:12